The Four Ends of the Greek Hyperinflation of 1941-1946

STUDIES IN 20TH & 21ST CENTURY EUROPEAN HISTORY

VOLUME 2

Edited by

Mogens Rüdiger and Mogens Pelt

University of Copenhagen

Michael Palairet

The Four Ends of the Greek Hyperinflation of 1941-1946

MUSEUM TUSCULANUM PRESS • UNIVERSITY OF COPENHAGEN

2000

Michael Palairet: The Four Ends of the Greek Hyperinflation of 1941-1946
Studies in 20th and 21st Century European History, vol.2

© Museum Tusculanum Press 2000
Layout and cover design by Henrik Maribo Pedersen
Printed in Denmark by Narayana Press, Gylling
ISBN 87 7289 582 9
ISSN 1398-1862

Published with the support of:
Unibank-fonden

Museum Tusculanum Press
University of Copenhagen
Njalsgade 92
DK-2300 Copenhagen S
Denmark

www.mtp.dk

Preface

Europe's first hyperinflation took place in France during the Revolution. The revolutionary governments resorted to the printing press as the only available means of financing the mobilization and feeding of vast revolutionary armies, so it may fairly be claimed that in 1793, the *assignats* - the inflation money of the period - saved the Revolution. However, the operation so severely damaged the French foreign credit as to contribute to France's eventual defeat in the struggle for European domination.[1] In any case, the *assignat* inflation provided a cautionary tale which was to discourage subsequent French and other European governments from abusing the monetary system too freely. Resurgence of hyperinflation therefore awaited the chaotic aftermath of World War 1, in Germany, Austria, Hungary, Poland and Russia. Because of advances in monetary theory, these hyperinflations - particularly the German case - have generated a lively literature since the 1970s. Most notably in the works of Webb, Holtfrerich, Feldman, Sargent, Ferguson, Boross, and Landau, old debates have been revived and reinterpreted through the adoption of neo-monetary and Keynesian stances.[2] World War 2 and its aftermath created a further crop of hyperinflations in Europe, in Greece, Hungary, and Romania. The second Hungarian case has been re-explored by Bomberger and Makinen and by Siklos, but because these inflations occurred in countries of lesser importance than Germany or Russia, they have received less attention.[3] Few economics texts on money devoted much more than a footnote to hyperinflation, since economists regarded it as a phenomenon borne of world wars and reparations, lying outside the normal range of monetary problems with which policy makers must grapple.

However, hyperinflation returned to Europe in the 1990s. In the case of Yugoslavia, it was certainly associated with war (though, if Mladjan Dinkić is right, it was caused principally not by war but by state corruption).[4] Yet neither war nor reparations were factors in the brief Bulgarian hyperinflation of 1996-1997. Nor were they an issue in the currency collapses experienced in Russia or Ukraine after the disintegration of the former Soviet Union. In Russia and Yugoslavia, a resurgence of hyperinflation still looks possible because the underlying causes of monetary instability have not been tackled satisfactorily. Hyperinflation therefore becomes an issue of more than mere historical interest. I came to the subject through teaching the economic history of interwar Europe, and developed a particular interest by following closely the monetary (and real) travails of Yugoslavia in 1989 and in 1992-4. In researching the subject with a view to creating a course on European hyperinflations, I found that the Greek case presented unusual features which invited further enquiry. Armed with some understanding of the theory (with which I open this study) I was puzzled as to how Greek governments between 1941 and 1946 could for a full five years finance their spending very largely from the printing press without their money being repudiated as a means of exchange. The book is, in broad terms, framed around this question.

An earlier draft of this book was very kindly read by Dr. Gail Makinen, author of several key econometric studies on the Greek inflation. His detailed comments have prompted me to make significant textual revisions, though we shall have to agree to differ over the impact on inflation of alternative currencies. But I remain intellectually in his debt. My thanks are also due to Edinburgh University Travel and Research Fund which assisted a brief visit I paid to the Bank of Greece in Athens, and to the staff in its library who could not have been more courteous and helpful.

Edinburgh, July 1999

Contents

Chapter 1.
    Introduction: Hyperinflation and stabilisation 9

Chapter 2.
    Defeat, Occupation and Economic Collapse (1941-42) 25

Chapter 3.
    The first "end" of the Greek hyperinflation: Neubacher's stabilisation
    and the "gold-action" 31

Chapter 4.
    Wages, living conditions and profiteering under Axis occupation 40

Chapter 5.
    Waley's stabilisation (November 1944) 51

Chapter 6.
    The Third "End": The Varvaressos Reform (June 1945) 76

Chapter 7.
    The fourth "End": The Anglo Greek Financial Agreement
    and its aftermath 87

Chapter 8.
    The four "ends:" An interpretation 96

APPENDIX
Monthly inflation variables, 1941-46 110
The price level (table A1) 110
The gold exchange rate of the drachma (table A2) 112
The money supply, M0 and M1 (table A3) 112
Occupation costs, Aug. 1941-Oct. 1944 (table A4) 114
Real wages (tables A6 and A7) 116

Table A1.
    Conversion of rent inclusive cost of living series to standardized
    consumer prices 118

Table A2.
    The gold price and the index of consumer prices in gold 125

Table A3.
    Money supply 128

Table A4.
    Greek occupation payments 1941-44 136

Table A5.
    Money supply and seigniorage 142

Table A6.
    Real wages and salaries in occupied Greece 148

Table A7.
    Real wages and salaries in liberated Greece 152

NOTES 153

BIBLIOGRAPHY 165

INDEX 169

Chapter 1. Introduction: Hyperinflation and stabilisation

In April 1941, Greece was subjected to Axis occupation and prices started to rocket. Hyperinflation began in June, when the price index advanced 52.3 percent on May. It peaked in force in October 1944, the month Greece was liberated, when prices rose by 7,459 percent. The inflation was not terminated till January 1946, so in all the Greek hyperinflation continued for 56 months. This probably makes it the longest such experience ever recorded. Over this period, prices compounded at 68.6 percent a month, causing the January 1946 price level to reach 5.1 trillion (5.1 x 10^{12}) times its level of May 1941. Inflation exceeded 50 percent a month in twenty months, and exceeded 10 percent a month in 43. If measured by the overall rise in prices from beginning to end of the hyperinflation period, the Greek inflation exceeded that of Weimar Germany by a factor of 5,000 times. It ranks third after the Yugoslav hyperinflation of March 1992 - January 1994, (1.94 x 10^{21} times) and the Hungarian hyperinflation of October 1944 to July 1946. [5]

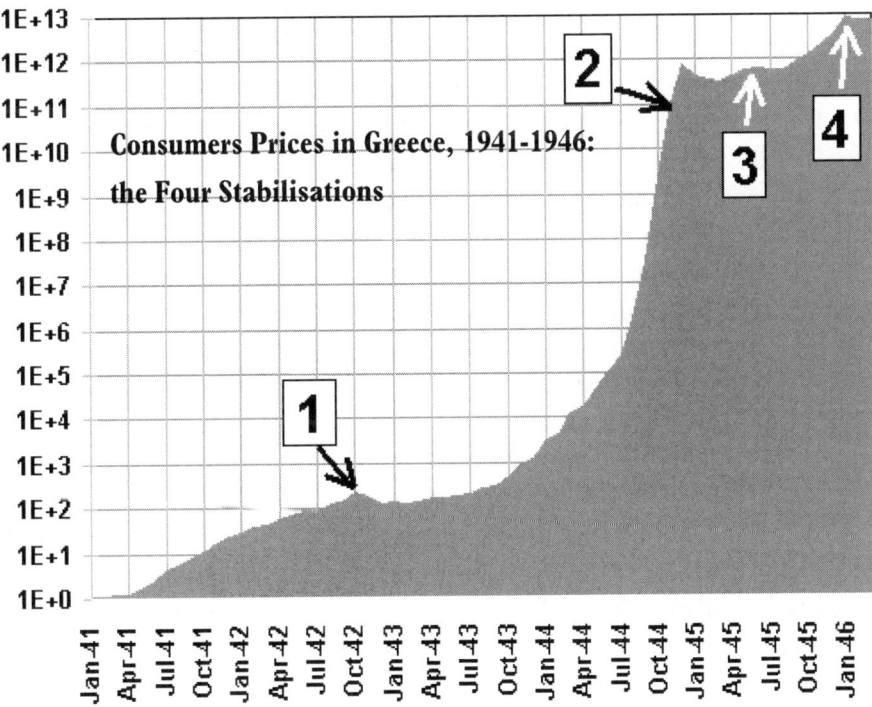

figure 1 (i)

The inflation process was, however, discontinuous, as indeed is characteristic of the course of all other European hyperinflations in the 20th century. Figure 1 (i) indicates the overall trend in consumers prices throughout the inflation period, and marks the onset of four periods of stabilization, all except the last of which proved to be transient. It is around these stabilizations that the study is constructed. The last three of these stabilizations were carried out during the post-liberation period, by the Greek authorities in co-operation with the British government. Although the pace of inflation was not allowed to reach the extremes suffered earlier under Axis occupation, the re-establishment of stable finances proved an almost intractable task. This study attempts to apply modern monetary theory to explain the course of the inflation and the failure of policy measures to bring it under control. It does not try to short-cut the political history of wartime and post-liberation Greece, but the nature of the subject does require us at the outset to introduce it through the medium of monetary theory, before applying this to the events of the hyperinflation period.

Modern hyperinflation theory developed out of a seminal paper of 1956 by Phillip Cagan. The statements made about the Greek and other inflations above adhere to his working definition of the phenomenon. He identified hyperinflation by its commencement during the first month in which prices rise by at least 50 percent and its cessation during the last month after which monthly price increases stay below 50 percent for at least one year.[6] Cagan's working definition of hyperinflation, though empirical, was grounded in analysis of the transactions demand for money. Most theoretical papers on hyperinflation follow a similar approach. The root cause of the Greek hyperinflation, like that of all serious inflations, was the excessive issue of new money throughout the inflation period in order to cover the deficits of the public authorities. The non-fiscal revenue raised this way is described as seigniorage. The loss to holders of high powered money through depreciation of the purchasing power of the money held is called inflation tax.

Heavy reliance on seigniorage - the printing of new money - to cover deficits is always inflationary. If, however, the public retains confidence that the balances it holds for current transactions will retain most of their purchasing power over the normal term across which it anticipates spending them, it will not diminish the desired real value of these balances so as to protect itself from the toll of inflation tax. On the contrary, it will let itself become more flush with liquidity than anticipated. It will be reluctant to reduce this liquidity because it expects prices to be higher in the future. So the relationship between the supply of transactions money and prices will remain at least stable, or even tend slowly to rise. Holders of money balances bear the burden of inflation tax, the loss they sustain from the erosion of their purchasing power, and the counterpart to the seigniorage secured by the authorities by printing money. The yield to the authorities from seigniorage at this stage therefore may exceed the apparent burden of inflation tax, because the real purchasing power of balances held by the public, as measured in current rather than expected prices, is tending to rise.

However, public confidence in the value of money can be weakened by a powerful shock to expectations, or by the sustained experience of paying inflation-tax at an unacceptably high rate. In this event, there comes a "break-point" into hyperinflation at which the rate of price inflation now overtakes the rate of creation of new money. This happens when the public, anticipating an unacceptably heavy exposure to inflation-tax, tries to reduce the real value of its fiat money transactions balances. Consumers convert their incomes as rapidly as possible into goods and services, while attempting to build personal inventories of less perishable goods in preference to holding fiat money. Traders reduce their transactions balances relative to their holding of merchandise. They raise prices (in so far as they are permitted) to decelerate the rate at which stock is depleted by sales, and they endeavour speedily to convert cash into new stock. If subjected to controls which prevent them from marking prices up, they attempt to reduce sales by withdrawing stock from the open market, and concealing it. They sell it, if at all, at "under the counter" prices.

These responses both by consumers and traders accelerate already high inflation. This forces the authorities to increase the rate at which they emit new money, as a proportion of the pre-existing money stock, in order to meet a given real deficit. The break-point can be used to define the transition to hyperinflation, as distinct from high or "Latin" inflation, during which real transactions balances are maintained. Beyond this point, the acceleration of inflation causes the public further to reduce the desired real balances on which it expects to bear the cost of inflation tax. So, if they need to maintain a constant real revenue from seigniorage, the authorities must raise still further their rate of emission.

This, in effect, imposes a rising tax rate on the shrinking inflation-tax base, which is composed of real transactions balances in fiat money.

The shrinkage of these real transactions balances is held by monetary economists to imply that the velocity of its circulation has speeded up. Velocity is measured through the Fisher equation. With this equation, measured change in the velocity of circulation (V) is defined by multiplying change in the price level (P) by change in the volume of transactions (T) and dividing the quotient by change in the stock of money, M. ($V=PT/M$)

It is at this point that we must register some reservations concerning the monetary theory of hyperinflation. This treats the volume of transactions as bearing a constant relationship to total output, which therefore stands as proxy for T. In hyperinflationary reality however, circulation almost certainly speeds up much less than measured "velocity". This is because transactions in fiat money shrink significantly under hyperinflation as a proportion of all transactions, and still more as a proportion of total output. Part of total output (mainly rural produce) retreats from the cash economy to subsistence provision. Moreover, it is likely there is a hyperinflation "break-point" beyond which the proportion of all transactions using fiat money suddenly contracts. So the observed "break point" (when real transactions balances in fiat money start to shrink) may be primarily attributable less to an absolute reduction in real transactions balances, than to the re-balancing of the public's transactions portfolio in favour of real values.

Within the traded element of total output, transactions in hard "alternative" currency or commodity monies displace those in fiat money, despite the illegality of such exchanges. Under extreme levels of hyperinflation, fiat money transactions at the retail level eventually become confined largely to perishable foodstuffs and to purchases of goods and services monopolised by the state. Traders become increasingly reluctant to sell non-perishable commodities for fiat money at any price. Employees try to compensate themselves by demanding part payment for their services in kind. So changes in the imputed velocity of circulation shown by the Fisher equation pick up both the extent to which the circulation of fiat money was really speeded, and the extent to which fiat money was displaced in transactions.

It is not possible directly to measure the extent to which the volume of fiat-money transactions fell during the Greek hyperinflation as a proportion of all transactions, for want of appropriate data. There is however reason to suppose that the "break point" - when real fiat money transactions balances started to shrink - coincided with a sudden shrinkage of the proportion of transactions financed by the circulation of fiat money, and a corresponding rise in the proportion of transactions financed by alternative currency and commodity money.

In this case, the principal force creating the "break point" may have been a sudden shift to the use in transactions of the alternative currency, rather than a sudden speed-up in circulation velocity. Evidence supporting this contention arises from P. Bernholz's study on the Soviet inflation in 1922-24, which aimed to measure the elasticity to inflation of substitution between inflationary and stable alternative currencies at very high rates of inflation. In this example, uniquely, the *chervonets*, a stable value alternative currency, was neither imported nor illegal, but was created by the Soviet state to circulate alongside the fast depreciating paper ruble or *sovznak*. Consequently, the state knew and published details of circulation of the *chervonets* as well as of prices expressed in *chervonets* terms, and the *chervonets-sovznak* exchange rate. Bernholz reports that the elasticity of substitution of the *chervonets* for the *sovznak* remained low at inflation rates of up to 30 percent a month. Depending on varied assumptions, 30 percent *sovznak* inflation caused a 19-23 percent substitution, but at 60 percent a month *sovznak* inflation, substitution leaped to 48-62 percent, and at 100 percent inflation, to 68-75 percent.[7] At 20 percent per month inflation in the *sovznak*, the alternative currency, the *chervonets*, accounted for 7-13 percent of M and would be hoarded. It therefore functioned as low powered money, accounting for a much smaller proportion of T than of M, while the *sovznak* would not be hoarded at all. Beyond this point, however, the public would not be able to hoard to a significantly greater extent, and so would use all the increment in *chervonets* as high powered money. In this (simplified) case, the alternative currency would finance zero percent of transactions at 20 percent per month inflation, about 10 percent of transactions at 30 percent, about 40 percent at 60 percent inflation, and about 60 percent of transactions at 100 percent inflation. Despite the awkward indivisibility of the *chervonets*, which created little obstacle to its hoarding, but which (intentionally) made it difficult to use as a transactions medium, substitution appears to have been very abrupt within the 30-60 percent inflation range, that is to say the range within which we should expect to find the break point.

In many hyperinflation cases, alternative currency will enter into circulation through dis-hoarding and import, but its volume might not suffice to displace fiat money to the same extent as in the Soviet example. In such cases, commodity monies become the only alternative quasi-monetary medium. How does this shortage of alternative currencies affect the transactions demand for fiat money? Theory insists that the lack of an escape route into hard currency would increase the demand for fiat money, for want of an alternative store of value, and therefore, other things being equal, this would cause a slowing of inflation. It was for this reason that the Austrian and German authorities during the 1921-1923 hyperinflations maintained *Devizenzentrale* systems to enforce exchange control and thereby increase the circulation of fiat money.[8] We doubt however that this had any such effect. Returning to the Soviet hyperinflation, Rostowski and Shapiro argue that the adoption of the *chervonets* did not reduce demand for the *sovznak*, since the *sovznak* was useless as a store of value, so nobody would hold it as such.[9] But suppose the *chervonets* had not been created. This would not have changed perceptions of the *sovznak* as a store of value, so different alternative currencies would have substituted. Most obviously, foreign exchange would have been imported. (The essential purpose of creating the *chervonets* had been to prevent this from happening). But, beyond this, the role of lower powered money would inevitably have been filled by commodity monies. Except for precious metals, which are themselves akin to foreign exchange, commodities of choice in hyperinflations have usually been single use goods, not durables. They included tobacco products, coffee, sugar, spirits and, very significantly, fats and oils. In Hungary (in 1946) when dealing in dollars was made too dangerous for traders, lard became the alternative commodity of choice, in Greece, olive oil, and in Yugoslavia, in 1992-1994, corn oil. In all these cases, fats and oils served as direct (though not, of course, exclusive) alternative media of exchange. Resort to single use commodity moneys (in the absence of alternative currency) would be more likely to speed inflation than to slow it, because it would necessitate the accumulation of otherwise unnecessary commodity stockpiles to serve as stores of value, leading to their consequent disappearance from authorized consumer markets.

The Greek hyperinflation offers a strong similarity with the Soviet experience. From 1943 at least, alternative currency, in this case gold coins, sovereigns and gold francs, circulated openly alongside the drachma, partly as a result of sales of gold by the authorities. Fiat money was being supplemented and displaced massively by the increase in the supply of gold coin. Gold became ubiquitous as a savings and transactions medium throughout the rest of the inflation and for many years after it. The so-called gold mania is usually held to have been undesirable as it promoted speculation that allegedly aggravated monetary instability. It is claimed to have prevented the normal regrowth of deposit money after the liberation, curtailing the ability of the banks to provide finance for reconstruction. The evidence we will present in Chapter 8 will however show that gold coin as alternative currency provided a vital lubricant for the Greek economic system, and that its availability permitted saving and reduced the pressure of demand on currently available merchandise supplies.

The sovereign was (nominally) of a value similar to that of the *chervonets*, and, like the *chervonets*, was not easily divisible. The implication here is that at around the "break-point" level of inflation, the elasticity of substitution of gold coin for paper money rapidly increased, and that beyond this point it rapidly displaced the drachma from circulation.

So while real transactions balances in fiat money shrank to tiny amounts during this (and any other) hyperinflation, fiat money, though circulating faster than in normal times, probably did not change hands at an extreme pace. Rather the public restructured its short term transactions portfolio so that fiat money comprised only a small component of it. This would suffice for purchases of goods and services in markets where fiat money remained acceptable in trade. A relatively rising component of the transactions portfolio was held in real values (gold or hard currency) which had formerly been held for hoarding.

A further part of the effective real money supply would be held in commodity monies. This would not have occurred if alternative currency were fully efficient as a substitute for fiat money. It occurred mainly because the alternative currencies were inaccessible to the public in quantity sufficient and units convenient to re-balance its transactions portfolios. Thus goods hoarding would also rise at around the 'break-point' inflation rate, in order to create a stock of barter commodities to supplement the supply of transactions money, in a similar manner to alternative currency. From this it follows that an insufficiency of alternative currency would increase demand pressure on the supply of commoditized goods. Conversely an increase in the availability of alternative currency reduced demand pressures, and therefore retarded the pace of inflation. Though neither changes in "true" velocity, nor in the structure of the transactions portfolio can be established independently from the normal range of officially collected statistics, they cannot be ignored, for they materially affected public behaviour under hyperinflationary conditions.

By associating hyperinflation with the significant shrinkage of the real (fiat) money balances held by the public, the period of hyperinflation can be re-defined (within Cagan's broader frame of reference) as beginning with monthly inflation at a rate sufficiently rapid to cause a month to month reduction in real money balances, and continuing for as long as these balances fail to revive and stabilise in the medium term, say, Cagan's 12-months. A revival of real balances over so protracted a period as a year can only happen if public finances are structurally reformed. More transient cessations of inflation which are unaccompanied by structural financial reform are not counted as successful stabilizations, even though they were brought about in the short term by the same means as longer term stabilizations.

We have taken this real balances framework for redefining hyperinflation, and applied it to the Greek case in Fig.1. (ii) below. This plots changes in the real money supply in Greece over the inflation and immediate post stabilisation periods. It indicates that real money balances tended to fall when inflation exceeded 42 percent a month. They fell in

Figure 1.(ii)

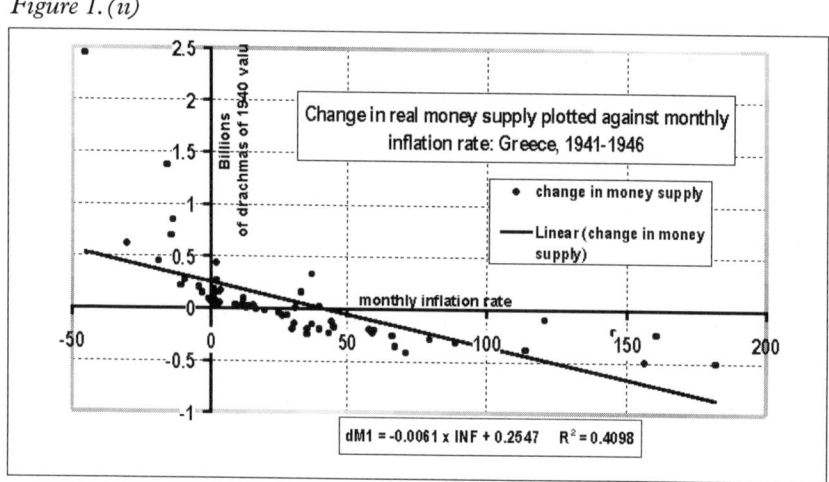

33 months out of 57. The longest interval in which real money balances rose uninterruptedly was of 10 months (November 1944 - August 1945.) This confirms that Greece experienced hyperinflation between May or June 1941 and January 1946. The Cagan definition, despite its apparently arbitrary choice of 50 percent a month inflation, and termination by 12 months of relatively stable prices, adequately defines the character and duration of the Greek hyperinflation.

Stabilisation

Over the period of the Greek hyperinflation as a whole, the rise in prices was discontinuous. For short periods, prices fell significantly, as between October 1942 and February 1943, between December 1944 and March 1945, and between June and July 1945. Similar sharp discontinuities in inflation trends are a common feature of all the great European hyperinflations. Monetary analysts cope with these discontinuities by building in changes in rational expectations on the part of the public, which cause sharp fluctuations in their preparedness to hold fiat money as opposed to merchandise.

This is so, but one needs to know why such expectations changes occur. Hyperinflations do not occur in a policy vacuum - on the contrary the authorities intervene continually, as a form of crisis management, and their interventions have significant short term effects. There exists in the hyperinflation literature a slightly unreal division of approaches between the "monetarist" and "structuralist" schools. Structuralists approach the subject in terms of the constraints placed on political choices which lead to hyperinflation. This is a reasonable approach, so long as it does not lapse into a facile determinism, which projects the political actors as impotent to avoid the outcomes which actually occurred. One must beware of the tendentious assumption that hyperinflation is associated with weak governments, whose leaders know what they have to do to stop inflation, but lack the power to implement the unpopular policies required to make stabilisation effective. This is not always true, for manipulating inflation could be applied as a useful discretionary policy option. Moreover, in the Greek case, the politicians concerned were loath to admit, in public at least, the causal relationship between deficit spending and hyperinflation. On the other hand, monetarists tend to be cavalier in researching the underlying political processes. There should be no basis for conflict between these "schools" if both the political processes and the monetary theory are properly integrated. The economist A K Lahiri has described monetarist analysts of hyperinflation as "structuralists in a hurry," and he is right. The present work insists on the need to integrate the structural with the monetary. Behind the fluctuations in prices and exchange rates we can usually discern the more or less visible hand of the state, seeking (within the constraints imposed by its revenue needs) to stop or at least decelerate inflation. Fluctuations occur because it is far easier for the authorities to initiate a stabilisation than to make it stick in the medium term.

Currency stabilisation results from a sharp reversal of inflation expectations, which creates a reverse "break-point." Traders must now want to increase their liquidity, by releasing pent-up stocks for sale, if need be by cutting prices, and by selling hard exchange. If they become confident that they can once more trade for fiat money without sustaining a replacement cost loss on their transactions, they will try quickly to rebuild turnover, if only because trading is the source of their livelihood, and hoarding was costing them current income. They will be under especial pressure to trade aggressively and to sell hard exchange if they are funding their stock with high interest debt, which now threatens to overwhelm them when repayable in stable money.

This signal from the trading community causes consumers to feel more confident that prices will stabilise in the short term, or at least that price rises will moderate, and that they can safely hold larger real fiat money balances as an adequate substitute for personal inventories. Simultaneously, fiat money becomes acceptable over a widening range of transactions. Therefore the price level is also depressed as the public restructures its transactions portfolio to meet the higher proportion of transactions it expects to meet in fiat money. To do so it dumps "real values" not just of merchandise, but also gold and foreign exchange. This puts upward pressure on the exchange rate, which in turn reinforces the stabilisation.

So to stabilise the currency, the prime task of the authorities is to engineer a situation in which traders put an enhanced supply of merchandise on the market, preferably cutting prices in order to clear it. To bring this sequence about, the authorities must make the public, above all the trading community, believe that government disposes both the means and the determination to bring inflation to an end, or at least very convincingly to reduce it. It is largely irrelevant whether or not it really disposes the means, or whether its proposed measures are theoretically sound and capable of effective implementation. Its prescriptions can be utterly wrong-headed, so long as they convince the public. The public does not necessarily associate hyperinflation with the loss of control by the authorities of the balance between their non-inflationary sources of income and their expenditures. Indeed, if it believes what the state tells it, it is more likely to attribute the cause of inflation to the machinations of hard currency speculators and greedy merchants. It is enough that the public now expects that the authorities can and will stop the inflation. This is because in the short term, as we have shown above, it is the public response to inflation news, not the operations of the authorities, which bring the stabilisation about.

Stabilizations are therefore achieved in the very short term, when the future conduct of the state is still uncertain. In the longer term, stabilisation will only hold if the authorities significantly reduce their reliance on emitting new money to a level at which inflation can be contained. This, of course, means bringing government and public sector spending more closely into line with revenue and receipts. In response, the public continues to raise its desired transactions balances to more normal levels. However, if the authorities fail to narrow the revenue gap, high inflation will re-ignite, and the stabilisation will be viewed retrospectively as having failed. This is what kept happening in Greece over the hyperinflation period.

Each of the falls in price during the hyperinflation period, as also a fall in prices in February 1946, occurred in response to short-term stabilisation measures. The first of the four stabilizations was carried out in October-November 1942, by Axis special commissioners Neubacher and d'Agostino. By the autumn of 1944, a renewed financial collapse had gained such momentum that a further stabilisation would have been attempted by the occupation authorities (or the issue of Greek money abandoned completely) were it not for their hasty evacuation of Greece in October. Thus a second stabilisation had to be carried out on 11 November 1944. It was executed according to a British Treasury plan hastily drafted by Sir David Waley. By April however, rapid inflation had resumed, so June 1945 saw a third stabilisation, by Governor of the Bank of Greece, Kyriakos Varvaressos. By September, the Varvaressos stabilisation in its turn collapsed. Renewed extreme inflation eventually prompted a "definitive" stabilisation, which was carried out on 24 January 1946. It was based on a financial agreement between the British and Greek governments. After this there was no return to extreme inflation levels.

This study is framed around these four stabilizations. The first three arrested the inflation for several months. The fourth promised no more lasting success than its predecessors, but was sustained by massive gold support for the drachma. Each stabilisation was contrived by holding out for the public the expectation (at least for the short term) that its holdings of drachmas would not rapidly be taxed away by inflation, as they had hitherto. They worked by causing the public tentatively to rebuild its real fiat money balances.

Most of the hyperinflations in twentieth century Europe were of relatively short duration, for if left uncontrolled, price rises would gather such momentum as to cause the increasingly widespread rejection of fiat money as recompense for the goods and services that the state and the public sector sought to secure by issuing it. Under the same extreme circumstances, it would also become virtually impossible to raise fiscal revenue, since its value would evaporate between collection and spending, a process referred to as the Tanzi effect.[10] This extreme was reached in Greece in April-November 1944, when 99 percent of government expenditure was uncovered by fiscal receipts.[11] In September to November of that year it became particularly difficult for the authorities to force the drachma as a means of payment. Under such circumstances, governments had to carry out some kind of stabilisation, whether they wished to or not, because without stabilising, they could be left without any purchasing power at all, either from fiscal sources or from seigniorage.

In the ideal stabilisation scenario, the authorities would use the period of grace afforded by this change of public expectations to realign their spending with their revenue (or vice versa). This would end inflation by removing its root cause. However, the Greek hyperinflation continued for 56-57 months across three stabilizations. During its course, as figure 8 (i) below shows, the authorities never ceased for a single month to meet their bills largely from seigniorage. (They also carried on doing so for 5 further months after the final stabilisation). So it is clear that none of the grace periods provided by the stabilizations were utilised to return to fiscal financing, and that the stabilizations became a mere device to perpetuate dependence on inflation revenue.

We therefore ask the "structural" question, why the Greek authorities were so long disinclined to procure fiscal revenues remotely to match their spending, preferring the expedient of printing money. This meant accepting the need periodically (and dishonestly) to restore confidence in the currency through the device of stabilisation. Even stabilisation itself was something they tried to defer till there was no alternative. With the exception of the Varvaressos reform of June 1945, all stabilisation attempts were carried out by foreign powers, or under their close supervision. Even Varvaressos' reform was only carried through after insistent British urging upon the Greek government. Except on that occasion, no government, either of the occupation or of the liberation period, made any serious effort to balance its spending with its revenue. The Axis occupiers and, after the liberation, British advisers repeatedly pressed the Greek authorities to carry out fiscal stabilisation measures, but usually won only lip-service from them.

The resistance of the Greek authorities to effective fiscal reform is by no means unique. The history of hyperinflation is papered with the wreckage of busted stabilizations preceding those which actually worked in the longer run. Such failures would never have occurred had it been as easy, administratively and politically, to carry through lasting public finance reforms as it was dishonestly to engineer transient resurgences of public confidence in the short term prospect of price stability.

The title of the present study is inspired indirectly by Thomas Sargent's comparative and theoretical study of the ending of four hyperinflations, in Austria, Germany, Hungary and Poland in the early 1920s. It acknowledges in particular the insights provided by Steven Webb in his paper on the "four ends" to the German inflation. There is however a significant difference of emphasis between these two papers. Sargent contends that "a dramatic change in the policy regime," in which "drastic fiscal and monetary measures" changed "the rules of the game" was required in all four cases for inflation to be overcome, and for stable currency to prevail.[12] Webb, however, demonstrates the capacity of hyperinflation repeatedly to be checked (but not terminated) by appropriate monetary measures.[13] True, the German stabilization of February

1923 must surely rank as the most "cosmetic" of all stabilizations, since absolutely no "convincing regime change" was offered, nor was any in prospect. It failed within weeks, precisely because of the absence of the appropriate reforms in public finance which could alone have secured mark stability. In their initial stages, however, both the German stabilizations of 1923 were similar in the pattern of public response to them. We will argue that the four Greek stabilisations were all more akin to the February stabilisation in Germany than to the November stabilisation, which actually held. The public did not have to take a view as to their prospective soundness.

*

After a review of the conditions which precipitated the initial phase of hyperinflation in Greece, we examine each of the four stabilisation programmes, their objectives and outcomes. Special attention is also devoted to real wage formation, because of the centrality of Greek official concern for the welfare of employees and their acquiescence towards government policies. This raises the question as to what extent if any wage-push contributed to the inflation process.

In concluding the study, we attempt to penetrate the mind-set of the Greek decision makers, to clarify why they behaved as they did. In particular, we examine their preoccupation with manipulating the rate at which the drachma exchanged against the gold sovereign (£ gold). We therefore review the effects of three official programmes for importing sovereigns, and for selling them through the Bank of Greece in order to support the drachma exchange rate.

This study utilises both quantitative and qualitative tools. For the former, we needed to establish viable monthly serials for the relevant monetary aggregates and indicators. Most of these serials required modification from the sources from which they were drawn. The data sets used in the present study also substitute the less satisfactory numbers used by Cagan. This causes our quantitative statements to differ materially from those generated by his brilliant analysis. For example, Cagan should ideally have applied as a measure of prices the best possible proxy for the GDP deflator, but for Greece he only disposed the Delivanis-Cleveland rent inclusive cost of living series. This indicator seriously understated the underlying trend in prices, because the cost of living was suppressed artificially, mainly by freezing house rents. The use of this unsatisfactory indicator of monthly average prices introduced distortions in his data which led him to date commencement of the inflation in November 1943, not June 1941. Moreover, Cagan ignored the continuation of hyperinflation beyond November 1945, for no apparent reason. Also, by using an index which recorded monthly price averages in conjunction with money supply figures for the end of the relevant month, when prices were usually much higher than their monthly average, his analysis gave birth to least one red herring (the need to explain a puzzling rise in the real money supply in September 1944, which never happened.) A more realistic, though still unsatisfactory measure of price inflation up to December 1944 is used in this paper (except where indicated otherwise.) This is the 1940 based S. Agapitides- N. Pizanias Athens area index of the cost of living, as recalculated with the rent element excluded. Thereafter, we have used the Bank of Greece cost of living index, also 1940 based, and again recalculated to exclude the house-rent element.

Our primary variables, for prices, exchange rates, money supply and wages, budgets and occupation charges were used to establish derived variables, mostly deflated to constant pre-war (1940) prices. These include the yield from seigniorage and real wages. Where un-annotated, textual references to the movements and values of basic and derived monthly financial variables are drawn from this data, which is set out in the appendix, together with sources and calculation procedures.

Qualitatively, the study rests both on the existing literature and on British Treasury, Foreign Office and Bank of England records. For the liberation period, they are exceptionally rich sources on Greek affairs, since at that time Greece was in all but name a British protectorate. Only one book, Delivanis and Cleveland, *Greek Monetary Developments 1939-1948* reviews the monetary history of the entire inflation era. Though now dated in its approach, it is nevertheless a vital starting point for research. The occupation period is less well served by the literature than the liberation. Essential reading includes accounts by two top German officials, Hermann Neubacher and Paul Hahn, both published in 1957. There is an excellent article in English based on these accounts by Harry Ritter, which is undeservedly buried in a *festschrift*.[14] A deservedly well received political history of the occupation period is Mark Mazower's *Inside Hitler's Greece*, but it is regrettably thin on economic and financial issues.

Probably the outstanding contribution for the post-liberation period is Gardner Patterson's Harvard thesis of 1948, which unfortunately remained unpublished. More than a detailed and scholarly thesis, it has some of the character of a primary source. Patterson, then a graduate economist, was present in Greece throughout the period of which he wrote, first as a US naval officer, then as US Treasury official. From the beginning of 1946 he served as an independent member of the Currency Committee for Greece. Of the contemporary memoirs, those of British Ambassador Rex Leeper, *When Greek Meets Greek*, were of particular interest. Leeper enjoyed near vice-regal powers in 1945 and exercised them relentlessly in trying to build up the Centre-Left as a "Third Force" in the country. He lamented that his "unpopular moderation" caused acute resentment and (on occasion) violent abuse. Leeper could take it: his arrival in the Greek Prime Minister's room, as he noted with satisfaction, could empty it instantly, as the crowds that milled round fled for the exits. His interventions, not least the making and breaking of governments in Greece, go to the structural core of the post-liberation inflation problem.

Notable recent work includes the examination of the economics of the hyperinflation in the series of articles by the American scholar Gail Makinen noted in our bibliography. The groundwork provided by Makinen's econometrics proved indispensable. For the liberation period, G. M. Alexander's *Prelude to the Truman Doctrine* stands as a reliable and well written political history, which, like Heinz Richter's left-leaning *British Intervention in Greece*, covers the financial issues extensively.

The British official documents are, on the whole, sharply critical of the actions, competencies and probity of the Greek officials of the liberation period. The author is aware that dependence on these sources may bias the conclusions of the study. However, the British themselves were between October 1944 and the end of the inflation the effective arbiters as to who should rule Greece, and to what ends they should rule it. So they - and Leeper above all - bear no small responsibility for the managerial failure which this study discusses.

Chapter 2. Defeat, Occupation and Economic Collapse (1941-42)

Greece was forced by Italy into World War II on 28 October 1940. Thanks to the foresight of the much reviled regime of Ioannis Metaxas (1936-41), Greece was able to confront Mussolini's troops with a strong and modernized military machine.[15] Resistance collapsed when Germany invaded in April 1941. The government fled into exile, thoughtfully taking out the gold reserve, and denied its successors access to the banknote printing plates as well.[16] During the period of active warfare between October 1940 and March 1941, the Metaxas government had resorted heavily to inflationary finance, procuring revenue by expanding the supply of primary money (M1) by about 1.933 billion drachmas of 1940 value per month. This enabled it to extract purchasing power at a monthly rate equivalent to about 35 percent of 1939 monthly domestic product, and in the process it expanded M1 by 46 percent.[17] Overt inflation was contained by large scale British financial and material assistance and by tough price controls, so prices advanced by a modest 14.2 percent between September 1940 and March 1941. In the light of subsequent events, it is interesting to note that the government of Greece at war extracted resources from inflation financing at 4.4 times the rate achieved by its successor during the Axis occupation, without as yet threatening confidence in the currency.[18]

With the breakdown of controls following the fall of Greece, the hitherto suppressed inflation became overt. In the 1920s inflation crises, the breakpoint into hyperinflation was only reached after protracted "Latin" inflation, but in the Greek case the shock to expectations that followed defeat and occupation plunged the country into hyperinflation within a month or two. The price explosion which followed was far more violent than could be attributed to the release of pent-up inflation. Between the beginning of the occupation in April 1941 and February 1942, prices rose by 3,079 percent. As early as June 1941 inflation exceeded Cagan's 50 percent a month hyperinflation threshold.

The explosion in prices was borne of economic collapse, which caused an initial violent shrinkage in the supply of goods available. The initial burst of inflation in occupied Greece was driven not only by the demand of the authorities for seigniorage but also by the intensifying shortages, above all of basic foodstuffs. An indicator of the worsening shortages is the price of commodities as measured in terms not of drachmas but of gold sovereigns. This indicator rose by 216 percent between May 1941 and February 1942. Supply side collapses had a role in precipitating all three of the more recent hyperinflations, as distinct from the hyperinflation experiences of the 1920s, when, if anything, aggregate supply was improving. The second Hungarian hyperinflation experience was similar to the Greek in being triggered by supply side collapse. (In Hungary, this occurred during the siege of Budapest in the autumn of 1944). Supply side shrinkages, caused by the disruption of intra-Yugoslav trade, also helped propel rump-Yugoslavia into hyperinflation in 1992.

The collapse in food supplies to the Greek cities in 1941 was caused by several mutually reinforcing pressures. Greece was cut off not only from her normal import of 600,000 tons of grain per year,[19] but also from her fertile northern provinces, which were annexed into Bulgaria. The 1941 harvest was disrupted by hostilities, and amounted to 70-85 percent of normal.[20] A disproportionately low fraction of this harvest reached the cities. Transport dislocations were partly responsible, but so too was the extreme reluctance of farmers, despite coercion, to surrender their grain. Since Venizelos' land reform of 1917, most farms were small peasant properties, not estates specialised to commercial grain production. The threat of a grain shortage caused the farmers to protect their subsistence needs by reducing sales. By artificially repressing the grain price, government aggravated this tendency. This resulted in hoarding by producers and intermediaries.[21] Some of the grain withheld from legal trade, however, found its way onto the black market, but its quantity was insufficient to ease supply. Shortages were worsened by the imposition on Greece of the feeding of the occupation armies. Besides this, the *Wehrmacht* exported intermittent food transports from Greece to supply Rommel's army in north Africa. The knowledge by Greek officials that the grain they collected from the farmers might be exported in this way encouraged the sabotaging of collection.[22] The meagre food rations actually distributed were partly imported from German occupied eastern Europe, Italy and neutral Turkey. The result of this acute grain shortage, together with the maldistribution of existing supplies was starvation, especially in Athens, during the terrible winter of 1941/2, when the sight of emaciated bodies lying in the streets became pitifully commonplace.

Though the acute shortage of supplies probably gave the initial stimulus to the escalation of prices, hyperinflation was sustained mainly by the massive creation of new money to cover public deficits. The price of gold sovereigns in terms of drachmas rose between May 1941 and February 1942 by 642 percent. The soaring public deficits stemmed not only from the unbalancing of formal budgets, but also the provision of subsidies to cover non-budget deficits, in particular those run up by the utilities and the commercial banks. Table 2.1 (see p. 34) tracks our estimate of the annual deficits of the Greek state through the occupation period. The most prominent item is the payments Greece had to make to the occupation authorities. By my estimate, in the 42 months between May 1941 and October 1944, the occupation forces collected about 12,600 million drachmas of 1940 purchasing power, or exactly 300 million drachmas a month, initially through the issue by themselves of military scrip, and subsequently through the issue to them of drachmas by the Bank of Greece.

These payments represented a heavy charge on the Greek economy. In 1939, Greece with a population of 7.2 million had generated a National Product variously estimated between 64.2 billion and 78 billion drachmas. The National Product estimates above were brought together by Freris, who regards none as satisfactory, but signals a preference for those at the lower end of the range.[23] In purchasing power parity terms, Greek National Product per capita in 1937 has been estimated at $92, about 27 percent of Germany's, but 13-23 percent above that of the other Balkan countries.[24] However, during the occupation, the remit of the Greek government and its currency extended over only about 60 percent of the pre-war population.[25] Partly for this reason, and partly because of the extreme dislocation of Greek trade, it is estimated (probably with a little exaggeration) that by 1942, the National Product of Greece had slumped to around 20 billion drachmas of 1939 purchasing power.[26] The burden of occupation charges seems therefore have amounted to around 20 percent of Greece's shrunken wartime National Product.

Greece was, by necessity, relieved of making significant military expenditures on its own account, so the net effect of their replacement in the budget by occupation costs was less severe than in gross terms. Rather it was the shrinkage of the tax base that set up acute fiscal disequilibrium. "By choice or necessity" writes Makinen, in discussing the causes of the inflation during the occupation years, the whole of the burden of occupation costs was met by the Greek authorities through the issue of new money, and not by taxation.[27] Makinen correctly identified the incapacity of the Greek tax system to generate revenue under inflation. He was taken to task by George Karatzas who argued that the authorities tried to "maintain a strong fiscal stance," but failed because of popular resistance to paying taxes to meet the expenses of enemy occupation forces.[28]

Karatzas' explanation is less than satisfactory. The approach of the Greek authorities to the fiscal problem was eccentric. Taxes on consumption goods were allowed to decay rapidly. So too were those on income. Pre-war, a pay-roll tax of 4 percent was deducted from government wages and salaries, and 5 percent from those paid in the private sector, but this tax was subsequently abolished.[29] New taxes substituted. The former tithe in kind was reinstated as a substitute for the land tax and as a means of extracting food from the peasants. But (to quote Stephen Xydis) "tax on the automatic super-valuation of real properties was most important, with the great demand for real estate: it was on a progressive and sliding scale reaching 60 percent and 50 percent respectively." A temporary tax was also levied "on extraordinary profits" at "50 percent on each unit above 20 million drachmas" while in June 1942 taxes were increased sharply on the professions and on "donations and inheritance."[30] Untangling this verbiage, it appears that the main target for taxation was the unreal capital gain created by the inflation of money values, instituting in effect a regular capital levy. Capital levies have a poor record during hyperinflations in raising revenue. They entail raising very large sums from a few individual tax-payers whose interests are likely to be so seriously damaged by such taxation as to force their tax affairs into the courts. The time lags for assessment and collection are long. Collectors can relatively cheaply be corrupted. The tax-payer has an incentive to delay payment for as long as he can. As the result of switching to this type of taxation, government unwittingly stripped itself of real fiscal revenues. It is still not clear as to why. The argument that allowing fiscal revenue to fall by a greater extent than was unavoidable represented some kind of passive resistance against the occupying powers is unconvincing, for it also reduced still further the discretion that the Quisling government enjoyed. It makes more sense when taken in conjunction with the analogous behaviour of its post-liberation successors. Greek governments, for their own political reasons, preferred to pretend that the whole nation, save only capitalists, could not afford to pay taxes. Among Greek politicians, only Varvaressos was ever to display any consciousness that inflation was a means of taxation, and was an arbitrary and regressive one at that.

Table 2.1 also shows the rising extent to which the government was expending funds to support economic activity. By 1943/4 subsidies were in magnitude more than twice as large as its own direct spending. This type of off-budget spending is inevitable during a hyperinflation. Inflation itself continually wipes out the value of business working capital, forcing farmers and industries into the bank merely to keep going. In 1943, some 70 billion drachmas had to be issued, mainly to the Agricultural Bank solely to finance the purchase of farm produce.[31] Utilities require massive subsidisation, not only because their prices are administered (i.e. suppressed) by the public authorities, but also because the charges levied on power and water can only be collected so long after their consumption that they are virtually distributed gratis.

The unrelieved dead weight of seigniorage financing rose from 78 percent of expenditures in 1941/2 to virtually 100 percent in the last six months of the occupation. As it represented a public sector deficit of 20-35 percent of national income, the explosive force of the Greek inflation can be no surprise. What should occasion surprise however was the ability of the authorities to extract a remarkably steady flow of seigniorage of this magnitude over so long a period. (See also table A5). Inflation, if left unchecked in the face of imbalances as huge as those shown in table A5 might be expected to destroy the functionality of fiat money as a medium of exchange in a year or less, and force a return to fiscal taxation. However, the Greek inflation machine relentlessly churned out purchasing power at 475 m. drachmas of 1940 value a month for occupiers, government and the business sector alike for 42 occupation months, without any semblance of a return to fiscal financing. It continued to provide revenues of 429 million drachmas a month for 21 further months following the liberation as well. Even in the last chaotic seven months of the occupation, when monthly inflation averaged 466 percent, seigniorage was still being extracted at 357m. 1940 drachmas a month. There was nothing accidental about this. How it was contrived forms the subject of the next chapter.

Table 2.1

Finance sources and expenditures in occupied Greece. (million drachmas of 1940 purchase power)				
	Apr. '41-Mar. '42	Apr. '42-Mar. 43	Apr. '43-Mar. '44	Apr. '44-Oct. '44
Income:				
-taxation	969	996	716	25
-seigniorage	6083	4131	7220	2496
Expenditure:				
-occupation payment	3820	2350	4781	1648
-civil government	2166	1716	1033	873 a
-subsidies	1067	1061	2122	
Total	7052	5127	7936	2521
percent by seigniorage	86.2	80.6	90.2	99
ditto (Delivanis-Cleveland estimate)	78	81	95	99

a. includes subsidies.

Notes. Seigniorage in 1941/2 includes my estimate for the issue of 1461m. drachmas (1940 value) equivalent in military scrip by Axis forces in May-July 1941, as well as 4622m. issued throughout the same fiscal year in drachmas by the central bank. (See below, p. 31) For estimates of drachma occupation payments by month, prices, and money issues, see tables A4 and A5. For government expenditures and subsidies up to fiscal 1943/4, see Bank of Greece, *Economic Situation in Greece*, p. 102. For April - Oct. 1944, the estimate of taxation as a proportion of spending is taken from Delivanis and Cleveland, *Greek Monetary Developments*, p. 94. Their estimates of seigniorage as a percentage of government spending are given in the bottom line of the table.

Chapter 3. The first "end" of the Greek hyperinflation: Neubacher's stabilisation and the "gold-action"

The supply-driven inflation which developed at the beginning of the occupation was quickly augmented by monetary inflation. This was largely but not exclusively caused by the burden on the Greek treasury of the costs of Axis occupation. During its initial stages (April-July 1941) the German and Italian armies in Greece lived off the land, the Germans issuing payment for what they took mainly in Euro-marks (RKKS) and the Italians in their Cassa Mediterranea and Ionian drachmas. The volume issued of this military scrip is unknown, but if it was used to extract resources from Greece at the same rate as in August to October 1941 (when the occupiers obtained drachmas from the Bank of Greece for this purpose) the real value secured by its emission would have been 1,461 million drachmas of 1940 purchasing power.[32] The issue of military scrip was a matter of short term expediency, for no new drachmas could be issued for some time from the government printing press. This must have been immobilised, because at the end of April 1941, as a stop-gap source of spending power, the new Greek authorities re-stamped and reissued an unknown quantity of worn notes, which had been cancelled and readied for destruction. When government note issues resumed in August, it was on the basis of a new set of note designs.

On the 5th and 6th of August 1941, new arrangements for financing the occupation were imposed by the Axis authorities on the reconstituted Greek government. Each of the occupation armies would draw payments of 1.5 billion drachmas a month from the Bank of Greece. This figure was fixed to extract the equivalent of one third of the pre-war budget of 12.5 billion drachmas, i.e. to produce for the armies about 350 million 1939 drachmas a month of resources.[33] In practice, in August about 4 billion drachmas were received by the occupiers - 728 million in terms of drachmas of 1940 purchase power. The occupation payments were supposed to cover the local content costs of supplying the armies, and to finance a programme of transport reconstruction and improvement.[34] From August 1941 till the end of the occupation, the Axis occupation authorities collected from the Greek government 11.14 billion drachmas of 1940 value in occupation costs, (or £8.26 m. gold) the Germans collecting 73.2 percent, the Italians the rest.

Early during the occupation the German authorities tried to get the Greek government to reform its system of tax collection, but wrote off the effort, such as it was, as unavailing. Therefore from the German point of view, the capacity of the Greek government to maximise its seigniorage was crucial to its ability to transfer resources to the Wehrmacht. German interventions into Greek monetary arrangements throughout the occupation have to be understood in this light. Only in this light are they fully comprehensible.

The initial hyperinflation of 1941 subsided somewhat after the new year of 1942. This was mainly because prices started to ease in terms of gold, indicating that the balance between supply and effective demand was improving. On the supply side, a trickle of imported grain was reaching Athens in neutral Swedish and Turkish ships. Effective demand had fallen drastically, at a new and miserably shrunken level of real wages, whose purchasing power was less than 12 percent of 1940. Occupation payments, as measured in constant drachmas, also eased from the unsustainably high levels of the early months. This may have been because the price of the drachma in gold was the basis for setting them at a time when, as shown above, the domestic purchasing power of gold had fallen dramatically. The occupation authorities were able to manage on a reduced flow of real resources because the loss was carried at the expense of the garrison troops. The pay of German occupation troops fell to derisory levels because of a fixed exchange rate applied between the (stable) Reichsmark and the inflationary drachma. According to Neubacher, "for his monthly salary, a general [stationed in Greece] could pay for one midday meal in a good restaurant."[35]

In the spring of 1942, the Bank of Greece moderated its emission of new money. Seigniorage fell from 570 million 1939 drachmas a month in Aug./Oct. 1941 to 275 million in Feb./Apr. 1942 and 318 m. in Aug./Oct. 1942. Occupation payments fell even more steeply from 487 million to 150 m. and 183 m. over the same period. Despite this, in January-October 1942, 62.1 percent of the yield from seigniorage was turned over to the occupation authorities. To supplement its dwindling regular revenue, the Greek government drew on forced loans from the banking system. However, the public tried increasingly hard to protect itself from inflation tax, by reducing its real money balances. Over the period from

October 1941 to October 1942, the real money supply fell by 72.6 percent. In the latter month inflation picked up to 59.2 percent.

An imminent currency collapse threatened. This would render worthless the flow of drachmas turned over to the occupation armies. From the German point of view, this was unacceptable. So far from easing its demands on the Greek economy, the Wehrmacht, in retreat from Alamein, was pressing for increased spending on fortification works in Greece, to guard against an allied invasion of Europe from north Africa. Moreover, allied commando and partisan activity was interfering increasingly with supplies from Germany. It was for these reasons that the first of the Axis interventions into the Greek financial system occurred in October-November 1942. The Greek economy had to be made more productive and more capable of releasing resources for the occupation powers to spend.

This need led to the establishment on 5 October 1942 of an Axis economic mission to Greece. To lead it, Hermann Neubacher was appointed on the 15th as Reich special commissioner. Neubacher, a foreign ministry economics specialist, was a Nazi of long standing, formerly mayor of Vienna and a top Farben executive. His remit was "to sustain Axis operations in Greece without destroying the Greek economy."[36] He was aware of the futility of getting the Greek client government to tax finance the occupation costs. Therefore his operation was essentially directed to reviving the capacity of the Greek monetary system to provide a medium term source of seigniorage.

This was to be done by indirect means. In Neubacher's view, little could be achieved by monetary policy, and priority had to be given to improving the civilian supply situation. In the short term, Wehrmacht expenditures in Greece would have to be cut back drastically, and civil imports expanded. He took advantage of an easing of the situation which was already being caused by the arrival of the first food transports supplied through Sweden by the International Red Cross (IRC). These transports were to provide a regular import of foodstuffs throughout the rest of the occupation. Neubacher arranged for these supplies to be augmented with 60,000 tons of potatoes, legumes and sugar, as a gift from the Reich (i.e. a German contribution to IRC effort). A smaller amount of pasta and sulphur was promised from Italy. Their availability should ease the pressure on food prices, but their arrival would take time.

Neubacher was, however, aware that the implementation of price controls had led to the accumulation of substantial secret and illegal inventories, "in caves and bricked-up cellars." Their release onto the market, if it could be secured, would bridge the supply gap till external supplies arrived. The simplest way to get these inventories released into trade, in the opinion of his superior Reich Foreign Minister Joachim von Ribbentrop, was "to have a dozen big speculators hanged."[37] Neubacher, a rare administrator who actually thought as an economist, decided differently. He agreed strategy with his Italian counterpart d'Agostino, on "the maddest war-economy heresy imaginable" - the abolition of rationing and the creation of a free market. This would secure the release of inventories more effectively than coercion, since the incentive to hoard inventories would be reduced if their price were no longer artificially restricted.

To induce the dis-hoarding of privately held stocks, Neubacher suddenly suspended payment to Greek contractors working on Wehrmacht and Greek government contracts. This squeezed their liquidity in drachmas. Anticipating that they would turn to the banks for accommodation, he also instructed the banks to restrict credit allocations. This would force the contractors to sell gold for drachmas, stopping the decline in the exchange rate, to which prices of free market goods tended to index themselves. The banks were also to use their own local knowledge and to squeeze merchants thought to hold concealed stocks, by stopping all payments except those financed by the depletion of inventories. To the same end, Neubacher also banned all export of foodstuffs. He acted quickly to sequester 600 tons of olive oil from Mytilene island, which had been bought by a German firm for export to Germany, and ordered it to be re-routed to Athens for sale on the open market.

The techniques worked, perhaps more successfully than the Commissioner himself had dared to expect. Prices suddenly broke on 14 November 1942. Inflation expectations diminished, and the public began rebuilding its transactions balances. Although the Greek government exploited the increased acceptability of the currency by pressing up the rate of non-fiscal taxation, the general price level (1940=1) descended from 229 in October to a nadir of 119 in February 1943, before rising back to 214 in July. During the same period the value of money balances rebounded from 1.36 billion 1940 drachmas to 4.11 billion (February) and 4.77 billion (July).

Neubacher followed this operation in December with the creation of the DEGRIGES. This was a German-Greek trade corporation. Its primary purpose was to provide occupation revenues from trade with Germany, at the expense of Greek importers, who had up till then enjoyed a windfall profit from the grotesque overvaluation of the drachma against the mark. This quasi-fiscal revenue source was however too small materially to to close the Greek government's deficits and the success of Neubacher's stabilization depended wholly on its non-fiscal elements.[38]

The nine months from November 1942 were, for occupied Greece, a time of relative prosperity and business animation. Factories began to reopen, and production to increase.[39] Over the occupation period as a whole, some 6,500 new enterprises were founded,[40] and it is likely their formation was concentrated within this period of relative ease.

Neubacher knew that the underlying disequilibrium in the Greek finances would ultimately sweep away the fragile stability his actions had brought about. For the longer term, he hoped "that the military development of the Greek theatre of operations would be concluded at the end of March 1943, and then a perceptible relief of the banknote press must occur."[41] He did not expect the Greek authorities to reform their finances. One must therefore conclude that, if military events in North Africa had moved in favour of the Germans, the Wehrmacht would have reduced its activity in Greece. The occupation levy it required would consequently have diminished.

In practice, the spectre of Allied invasion from North Africa caused the Wehrmacht to press up its demands for Greek resources to build fortifications, U-boat pens, roads, airfields and shore batteries. Occupation costs which had been contained (by my estimate) at 257.3 million 1940 drachmas a month between January and April 1943, soared to an estimated 589.3 million between May and August. Neubacher attributed the renewed resurgence of hyperinflation to this intensification of occupation spending, which he was unable to resist.[42] The ending of the Italian occupation in September eased the bill for occupation payments from the Bank of Greece. Its credits to the Italians had been running at about £200,000 (gold) a month, not far short of the £260,000 (gold) the Germans were themselves spending. The Germans did not press up their own demands to compensate. This should have eased inflationary pressures, but the Greek government was rapidly pressing up its own uncovered expenditures in the latter months of 1943. So although real occupation costs overall subsided to 338.4 million drachmas of 1940 in September - December, the collective hunger of the authorities for seigniorage remained at levels which it would be impossible for long to sustain.

Monthly inflation speeded up from 15.8 percent in September 1943 to 79.7 percent in November. This was accompanied by a renewed 47.6 percent shrinkage in the real (fiat) money supply. The Wehrmacht encountered increasing difficulty in its procurements. Therefore the Germans were forced once more to change financial tactics in Greece before the capacity of currency issues to finance occupation costs evaporated. Neubacher had toyed with a plan to halve the real money supply by bisecting notes in circulation, returning the holder one half over-franked to half its face value, and retaining the other half to finance future occupation spending. He rejected it, on the grounds that the operation was not repeatable.[43] Though the plan was put up by a German banking expert, a similar scheme had, curiously enough, already been applied in Greece, in 1922 and had been repeated there in 1926.[44]

Neubacher was, however, nothing if not innovative. He flew to Berlin in November to argue that more resources must come from Germany to sustain the occupation. As partisan activity was causing acute supply difficulties, he proposed that gold should be released to facilitate Wehrmacht purchasing. He quickly won the assent of the economics ministry and the Reichsbank to the release of one million gold sovereigns for this purpose.[45] The sovereigns were already in Athens, physically stored at the Bank of Greece, for they had been brought in between February and September.[46]

The Wehrmacht had expected to use this gold for direct payment to its contractors, but Neubacher calculated it could be more efficaciously deployed to support the currency. The Wehrmacht would continue to pay its bills in drachmas. The gold would be auctioned on the Athens Stock Exchange (now reopened for this purpose) and the Wehrmacht would receive and spend the drachma counterpart funds generated by these sales as well as the credits supplied by the Bank of Greece. The gold sales in themselves would steady the drachma-gold exchange rate, slowing the rate of price increases, and restore a modicum of confidence in the currency. Note printing would therefore continue to yield a significant volume of seigniorage, at the disposal both of the Wehrmacht and the Greek government. These revenues would be lost to both parties if the Wehrmacht moved to gold payments, since (in Neubacher's view) local currency would simply be refused as a means of payment. This would happen not only in Greece but also in neighbouring occupied states, where contractors would also demand gold payment.

The Reich "gold action" began in November 1943 with the sale of 20,000 sovereigns on the Greek market. Astonished Greek businessmen started to question, should we be buying gold, or selling it ourselves? The gold supply at Neubacher's disposal was limited, and its essential function was to preserve the drachma as a seigniorage source for as long as possible. To re-stabilise the currency outright would be too costly. Therefore Neubacher and his subordinate Paul Hahn engaged in a protracted tactical game against the market, selling, and on occasion buying, sufficient gold to change short term expectations, and to slow the inflation rate. It was a dirty game they played: several times they repeated the operation of November 1942, suspending payment to Wehrmacht suppliers and freezing bank credit for up to ten days at a time. This was done to force businessmen to sell gold, and so to provide "a crude but effective form of currency support" at their own expense.[47] The Wehrmacht disliked the system, because it reduced its credit-worthiness with suppliers in Greece, who tried to match new supplies with payments. However, the numerical data support Neubacher's contention that by supporting the drachma the Wehrmacht extracted far larger supplies from Greece than could have been procured through gold payments alone.

During the period November 1943 - October 1944, the German authorities, by my calculation, sold £1,122,552 gold for drachmas. This corresponds roughly with Hahn's account, showing the sale over the gold action period of 763,519 sovereigns and 11,265,770 gold francs, or £1,214,150. Additionally, they drew the drachma equivalent of £2,049,534 gold in occupation payments from the Bank of Greece. Assuming that the "gold action" prevented the drachma from collapsing outright, and therefore preserved it as a source of seigniorage, it enabled the Greek note press to yield the Wehrmacht some 64.6 percent of its occupation spending (the gold action, 35.4 percent). The Greek government also continued to receive non fiscal revenue.

This gain was not offset by any consequent dilution of the (indirect) purchasing power of gold. The Germans obtained goods and services for their gold worth 1,386 drachmas of 1940 per sovereign (or gold franc equivalent) expended. In 1940 the drachma had exchanged at 1,100 to the sovereign[48]. Assuming that the price of the goods and services they procured in Greece advanced broadly in line with the general level of Greek prices, then considering the acute shortage environment in which they operated, the Germans were buying from Greece on highly advantageous terms. This was not the result of a conscious policy, rather because the volume of gold they sold was insufficient to dent the high real price that the Greek public was willing to pay for gold.

The alternative way of obtaining supplies in the absence of a local currency capable of yielding seigniorage would have been coercion. This would have suited Hermann Göring, an opponent of Neubacher's "shit-currency" policy.[49] But by 1944, the Germans could not afford further to alienate Greek sympathies, as the partisan movements were fast extending the area under their control. Neubacher himself encouraged the Rallis government to recruit security battalions to contain the damage. The need to finance this expenditure probably explains his concern to protect the access of the Greek authorities to seigniorage revenue.

By August 1944, inflation reached 534 percent a month, and the value of the drachma money supply contracted to 3.6 percent of its June 1943 peak. The yield from seigniorage remained remarkably robust, at 275 million drachmas of 1940, but Neubacher's gold supply was running low. Without further heavy gold sales to decelerate its collapse, the drachma could not much longer be counted on to yield seigniorage. So at the end of the month, Neubacher attended a Führer conference at Rastenburg to ask for more gold.

Hitler was sceptical about releasing it, though he recognised the desirability of preserving the drachma as a source of seigniorage. He suggested that Neubacher create a *"Rentendrachma"* along the lines of the post-stabilisation *Rentenmark* of 1923. The *Rentenmark* had been introduced in Germany as an inconvertible but stable value interim currency in November 1923, to stop the German hyperinflation. The government had been granted a loan from the Rentenbank, to tide it over while the budget was being re-balanced. This amounted to an advance on the seigniorage to be reaped from the willingness of the public to rebuild its transactions balances. Despite its lack of convertibility, confidence in the future stability of the *Rentenmark* enabled the authorities to maintain its value[50]. A similar operation in Greece would theoretically produce an analogous harvest of seigniorage - provided the public could be induced to hold *Rentendrachmas*.

Neubacher thought it could not. He objected that "it would not work for a quarter of an hour, that is to say for the time it took for the first Greek to demand gold at the bank of issue for such a [*Rentendrachma*] note." Hitler persisted in his proposal, so Ribbentrop (unsuccessfully) pressed Neubacher to launch the scheme.⁵¹ Neubacher returned to Athens empty handed, but continued to make token gold sales up to the first week in October, before turning over the residual £12,628 gold to the Wehrmacht in cash.⁵² By then the Germans were evacuating Greece, wrecking communications in their wake to avoid being cut off from Germany by Russia's Balkan offensive. The *Rentendrachma* scheme, though never applied, was entirely consistent with German policy since the beginning of Neubacher's mission: to maximise the capacity of the Greek currency to yield seigniorage.

Chapter 4. Wages, living conditions and profiteering under Axis occupation

During the disastrous early period of the occupation the supply crisis caused heavy excess mortality in the cities. In peacetime per capita bread consumption had been 406 grams per day, but between October 1941 and March 1942, bread rations in the Athens - Piraeus area averaged a sub-survival 116 grams, reaching a nadir of 84 grams in February.[53] Mortality figures for Athens and Piraeus showed 14,566 deaths in the year October 1940 - September 1941, and 49,188 deaths in the twelve subsequent months. The figures understate the rise in mortality because of the incentive to families conceal deaths and retain the ration cards of the deceased.[54] Thanks to IRC food relief, conditions during the rest of the occupation were less acute than those experienced that first winter, though its activities were largely confined to the cities, and localised famines were to recur, especially where counter-insurgency operations interfered with supplies. Not all of the food was distributed to optimise humanitarian efficiency. Aid organisations have to bend to the demands of armed combatants. The German authorities were convinced that ELAS - the guerrilla arm of the Communists - and the British Special Operations Executive (SOE) exploited the aid programme to their own advantage, while Greek sources argue that the Germans did likewise.[55] Under these conditions, the level of real wages fluctuated wildly, between rates sufficient to provide a tolerable adequacy to rates that signal the most wretched depths of poverty.

Figure 4 (i) attempts to track the performance of real wages and salaries across the hyperinflation period to the end of 1944. Relying largely on data compiled by Agapitides, and adjusted for wages payments in kind from February to November 1944 it can make no claim to accuracy. It is based on wage tariffs which were fixed by law but were frequently revised. We know that wages and salaries actually (though illegally) paid were at most times significantly larger than those officially recorded. Nevertheless, the fluctuations shown are sharp and extreme, and may be treated as a guide to the underlying realities.

The initial food crisis was attended by a collapse in real wages. By October 1942 unskilled real wages had sunk to 8 percent of 1940, the wages of government clerks to 14.4 percent, and of private employ-

Figure 4 (i)

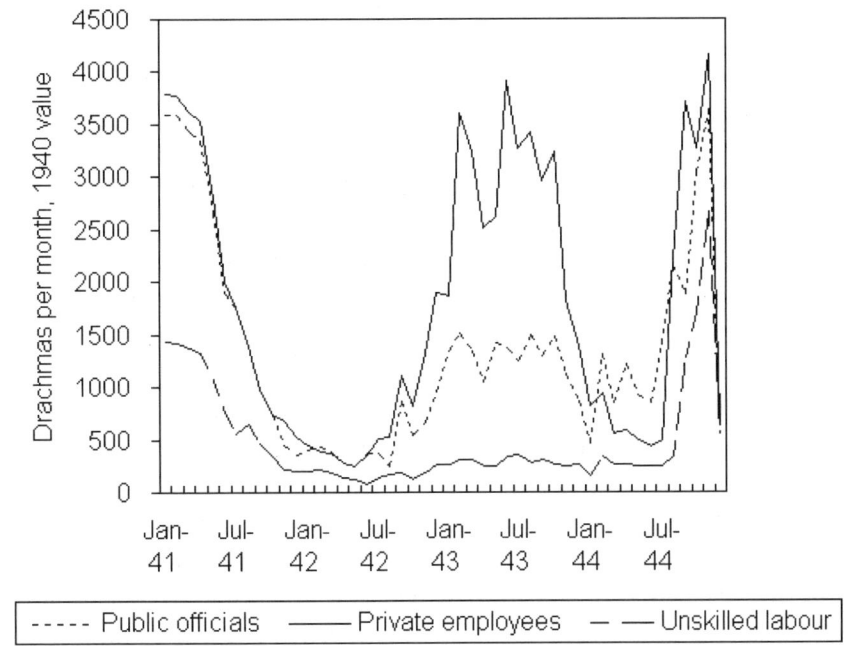

Source: *table a6.*

ees to 20.5 percent. This was the background to Neubacher's decision that the control of inflation required the alleviation of living conditions if Greece were to continue to supply resources to support the Wehrmacht.

The combination of the inflow of relief supplies and Neubacher's reform transformed the picture, not merely in monetary terms, but in welfare terms as well. Government clerical wages rebounded in February 1943 to 39.6 percent of 1940, those of private employees to 90.2 percent and unskilled wages to 20.8 percent.[56] The recovery was transient, but as figure 4 (i) shows, wages more or less kept pace with prices till November 1943. They then entered a renewed and precipitous descent. Nevertheless, the regular delivery of about 18,000 tons a month of IRC food aid, and the pressing demand by the Germans for labour, which absorbed the services of about 200,000 Greek workers,[57] prevented social conditions from returning to the famine levels of 1942.[58]

The recovery in tariff salaries following the Neubacher reform, as depicted in figure 4 (i), was far stronger in the private sector than in the state institutions. The tariff wages of manual labourers remained extremely small relative to pre-war. In reality, however, trends in real wages in all three categories were probably similar. The experience of most wage and salary recipients approximated more closely to that shown for private sector employees than that recorded for other groups. This is because private sector employees, at least in 1943, received "practically no allowances" to supplement their nominal salaries, but both civil service and manual wage tariffs were heavily supplemented. An extreme example of supplementation was the case of a clerk at the Bank of Greece. He drew a basic salary for August 1943 of 250,000 drachmas, which was paid him monthly *in advance*. A range of allowances advanced his total receipts from employment to 1.37 million drachmas or 5.5 times his basic salary. His family therefore lived "as far as such simple foodstuffs as are available is concerned, almost as well as in 1940," though it could not afford to purchase clothing or footwear. The position of Bank of Greece employees was exceptional: their employer did after all print the money concerned. Only very privileged groups, including employees of the state owned banks and of the railways, received similar largesse. The banks themselves did not make money out of the inflation: on the contrary, they were effectively bankrupted. The National Bank considered its prime duty "first to provide food and the vital necessities to its staff." The "scandalous differentiation" existing between the employees of all four of the big banks, and other staff led to legislation limiting the assistance these people could be given.⁵⁹ Other civil servants fared less well, but even these were granted advances equal to 2-3 months pay to ease their distress.⁶⁰

The tariff scales for manual day wages were so low during the occupation, even during the most favourable period, that they had to be supplemented massively. From late 1942 onwards, manual labour was much in demand for fortification and communications work. The prevalence of informal (and illegal) supplementation is verified by refugee de-briefings. The unskilled wage tariff according to Agapitides was (assuming a 26 day working month) about 28,100 drachmas in May 1943, 51,500 in August and 65,500 in September, but British intelligence reports signalled around 125,000, 342,000 and 440,000 respectively or 4.4 times, 6.6 times and 6.7 times tariff. These figures imply real levels of 73, 123 and 138 percent of the pre-war norm.⁶¹ These "real" unskilled wage figures are too few and too imprecise to be embedded in our analysis, and they may include fringe benefits which were also customary before the war. However, the general range of experience in summer 1943 was probably close to that indicated by the trend in private employee tariff wages, with civil service and unskilled manual tariffs seriously understating real wages in this relatively prosperous period.

Real wages collapsed in the winter of 1943. Using the Agapitides figures, their unweighted index slid from an index figure of 47.8 percent of 1940 in August 1943 to 14.3 percent in January 1944. This gave rise to an upsurge of claims for wage payment in kind, which were backed by E.A.M., the Communist dominated National Liberation Front. These demands were conceded increasingly by employers, though the practice was illegal.⁶² Eventually the Greek government ordered employers with effect from 1 February 1944, to supplement tariff wages with a monthly bonus in kind worth the equivalent of 194 pre-war drachmas. It raised the bonus to 323 drachmas equivalent on 13 September, and again to 451 drachmas equivalent on 1 October. Additional allowances were also made for certain categories of worker.⁶³ The bonuses were composed of local produce, such as olives, vegetables, cheese, fish, figs, and charcoal. Compared with unskilled monthly wages in 1939 of about 1,500 drachmas a month, the bonuses were not large. However, they supplemented the relief rations, which were purchasable "practically without charge," while house-rents were "effectively eliminated" by rent control. The September and October 1944 allowances should probably be interpreted as desperate populist gestures by the Rallis government in the face of imminent collapse. In Figure 4 (i) the officially conceded payments in kind are added to the tariff wage rates from February 1944.

For 1944, we have no means of cross-checking the Agapitides tariff figures. After adjustment for statutory payments in kind these figures indicate a renewed slump in pay by June 1944 for government clerks to 22.3 percent of 1940. Private employees' pay fell to 11 percent, and that of the unskilled to 15.8 percent. Conditions in the summer of 1944 were exceptionally bleak. The IRC food deliveries maintained a "relatively adequate" bread ration, but ordinary commerce ground to a standstill for want of commodities. Olive oil all but vanished from the market. In Athens the only branch of commerce to flourish was the trade in second-hand goods and antiques, on the proceeds of whose sale many Athenians came to depend.[64]

It may even be questioned whether the food wage schemes of 1944 were of real avail to wage and salary earners. In the medium run, real wages would ultimately depend on the resources available to feed the civil population, regardless of whether these were made available through the exchange mechanism, or through direct allocation. At this time, however, real wages and consumption standards probably continued to be sensitive to changes in foodstuff inventories, just as they had been in late 1942. The violent acceleration of inflation in the autumn of 1943 would have caused merchants to cut back supplies of non-perishables to the market, because of the losses sustained in holding money while replacing inventories. Moreover, inventories (above all of olive oil) provided a negotiable store of value, in an economy where the supply of alternative stable value assets was small.

A strange turn of events in the latter part of 1944 tends to confirm this reckoning. We showed earlier that between May 1941 and February 1942, the price index rose from 100 to 316 when expressed in gold terms. Though imperfect, this index of commodity price trends relative to gold is the best available barometer of variations in shortage of goods whose demand elasticity was low. From February to October 1942, this index slid back to 148.5, after which it fluctuated around a falling trend to May 1944, when it reached a nadir of 104.9. Most of this secular fall was concentrated between January and May 1944. It probably reflects the relatively heavy gold sales of this period. Thereupon, however, this index rose steeply, to 398.5 in September. An increasing shortage of domestic farm produce is reflected by the soaring price (in gold) of olive oil, 25 oka (32 kg.) to the sovereign in 1939, 6 oka early in 1944, 3 in the autumn of that year.[65] By the time the Allied advance troops landed in October, all food was outrageously expensive - even in dollars.[66]

This was not an environment in which one might expect real wages to have recovered or even to have been maintained. Perversely though, between June and September 1944 the (unweighted) index of the three real wage types began to soar. In August, it was back at 44.9 percent of 1940, close to the level attained in the spring of 1943. In September it reached 75.8 percent of 1940, in October, 91.6 percent. The implication is that the general shortage of goods in the last months of the occupation was caused, not by a worsening in supply, rather by the growing pressure of effective demand.

One could alternatively dismiss this supposed dramatic recovery in real wages as the artefact of a dubious statistical serial which we have already questioned in respect of the 1943 data. In one respect it is certainly over-optimistic. According to a British foreign office report compiled soon after the liberation, and intriguingly labelled "not for publication or to be seen by Greek nationals," many official wages and salaries fell into arrears, and therefore would have been worth little when finally they were disbursed. This however was more a problem in the provinces than in Athens, and outside Athens both the inflation rate and the absolute level of prices were far below those ruling in the city.[67]

The soaring level of real wages is however indirectly affirmed from contemporary qualitative evidence. A sliding scale of wages, linked to a cost of living index, was applied from September onwards to payment of all wage earners, private as well as government. Reportedly, it "led to wage revisions every few days as the cost of living advanced." This index was based upon the black market price of 16 items considered essential to supplement Swedish-Swiss IRC ration distributions. Indexation in itself cannot cause wages to lead inflation except when inflation is falling, but it was later claimed that wages were automatically over-indexed. Many index items had become too expensive to be consumed in significant quantity.[68] Some were "virtually unobtainable at any price." So their inclusion in the index caused money wages "always" to outstrip the prices of goods which actually entered into commerce.[69]

There is further evidence that real wages, at least in the public sector, had risen unduly. Four days after its installation in Athens, the liberation government, devoid of means for meeting the civil service and public utilities payrolls, begged for IRC assistance with the delivery of supplies so as to be able to pay these employees in kind. The British army was sympathetic to the request. However, the IRC team on the spot was led by a Swedish politician, Dr Sandstrom, who had experience of local conditions over a longer period than the in-coming liberators. The IRC representatives were less than overwhelmed by the plight of the relatively affluent employees that the government sought to help, in a country where stark destitution was horribly prevalent. They said they had not supplies available on the requisite scale. They "added somewhat bluntly that those concerned must in consequence face a lower standard of living."[70]

The surge in wage-driven demand was made effective by several mutually reinforcing pressures. The food-wage system itself contributed. Large numbers of persons, especially family members of the already employed, were inscribed onto pay-rolls to give them access to the food entitlement.[71] So too did the wage indexation system. But both these devices were clearly a response by an increasingly insecure Greek government to the demands of a labour force which was heavily penetrated by E.A.M., and which felt increasingly confident of its ability to exploit its political power.

The food wage system and wage over-indexation as devices to increase mass purchasing power should have driven the price of un-allocated food to prohibitive levels. Yet, clearly, this did not happen, for increased supply must have been released on to the market, or else real wages could not have risen as they did. Whence were supplies augmented? The only possible source was the depletion of inventories, a process analogous to that which had occurred in the winter of 1942. With the resurgence of hyperinflation in late 1943, traders had withdrawn goods from the market, to minimise their exposure to inflation tax. The widespread knowledge that inventories were again being hoarded (as they had been under the price-control regime of 1942) and the not unjustified belief that this was again causing the purchasing power of wages to collapse caused a sharpened public resentment against business.

The response may be found in a reference by Thomadakis to "labour struggles" and the inter-related activities of the guerrillas. The looting of food shops became frequent from the end of 1943. It was not spontaneous, but organised by E.A.M.-ELAS, which attacked commercial food inventories and redistributed them at low prices.[72] Moreover, the partisans took "harsh measures against profiteers," in rural areas under their control. They threatened merchants with death if they did not sell merchandise at the prices they themselves established.[73] By the summer of 1944, pressure from ELAS had strengthened so much that traders faced an increasing risk of politicised food looting, and feared an imminent Communist seizure of power. In the chaotic twilight period while the Germans carried out their staged evacuation of Greece, organised economic life in the capital came to a standstill. Power, light and urban transport were shut off. Since food was "expensive and difficult to get," E.A.M. was active in its efforts to decrease the prices of essentials. As its guerrillas had established effective mastery of the suburbs, it is reasonable to suppose that their methods were effective. Business responded negatively. The bakers went on strike and many shops closed.[74] Even after the liberation, a telegraphic message claimed "Drachma reported valueless/ business at standstill/ shops closing/ raiding of shops and demonstrations."[75]

The attacks on business demonstrated all too clearly to traders the unwisdom of continuing to withhold inventories from the market, rather than to sell them at below market price. It was also not necessary. Businessmen could, if they were wise, carry on trading and depleting their inventories at minimal loss, because their wealth no longer had to be held in the form of merchandise. This was thanks to the "gold action," and the heavy spending of gold by British agents to secure partisan cooperation. The much increased accessibility of gold coins offered merchants a convenient and secure means of converting inventories into notionally stable values, even though the purchasing power of the gold they bought was falling relative to the goods they sold. Despite their obvious reluctance to accept dictation from the guerrillas, the fact is that businessmen were reducing inventories and acquiring gold in response to the prospect of the German withdrawal. This is noted by Delivanis and Cleveland.[76] They explain that merchants expected the withdrawal to cause a slump in demand, while labour needed to be paid increasingly in specie not money. This would reinforce the pressure to unload inventories, and therefore reduce goods prices relative to wages.

The response by businessmen both to the security risk and the trade risk would explain the fall in real merchandise prices relative to wages, parallel with a rise in the price of merchandise relative to gold. The result, according to reports for October 1944, was an absolute collapse in inventories. The depreciation of gold in terms of goods as a result of the extreme goods shortage tended to force business back to barter,[77] but it may be surmised that the shop closures reported resulted less from a desire by their owners to withdraw inventories from the market, which was dangerous, but rather because they had sold out of stock and could not replace it.

We conclude that the expectation of German withdrawal led to a panic release of merchandise, and that this gave rise to a transient boom in real wages and consequently consumption. This was to lay up trouble in the early phase of the liberation, for the resources available could not long support the maintenance of this consumption level.

Over the period of the occupation, the living standards of employed labour, their dreadful descent in 1941-42, their revival during the winter of 1942/3, their renewed fall in the winter of 1943-1944, and their spectacular recovery in the autumn of 1944 were primarily the result of violent adjustments in the volume of trade inventories. This was to remain the case during the liberation period as well.

It is an article of faith among writers on the occupation period that almost the whole Greek nation was reduced to penury or worse, while business people prospered by collaborating with the occupation forces. As we have seen, the experience of wage and salary earners was diverse, geographically, occupationally, and over time. The latter part of the statement is hardly more secure. It was fuelled largely by the Marxist tenets shared by Greek intellectuals, and their class antagonism to business. After the liberation, left-leaning governments were to take keen interest in the issue of profiteering during the occupation, because it offered the prospect of gouging large quantities of revenue without pain to the majority. As prospective taxpayers, "war profiteers" never fulfilled expectations, possibly because the fabulous profits made during the occupation were partly mythical.

An obvious target was the property speculator, in particular the purchaser of property on mortgage credit. Property turnover during the occupation was brisk - some 350,000 properties changed hands for £6 million (gold) - but this was driven mainly by distress selling in a collapsed market. In terms of gold, the mean transaction price was a mere

6.7 percent of pre-war.[78] The distress which drove these sales resulted from the rent freeze. A report of 1944 noted that "conditions of owners of real estate, because of legislation limiting the price of rents, has become so serious that the government has been forced to give them relief in cash to enable them to live."[79] Those who sold up "to keep alive" found their pitiful proceeds subject to ferocious taxation on the nominal capital gain they realised, which concealed a real and massive capital loss. Since the purchaser would likewise incur huge taxes on disposal of the asset, and could not draw in rent enough to cover its maintenance, there was little competition to buy. Obviously some buyers would reap rewards after the liberation when controlled rents were pitched at less unrealistic levels, and therefore they would become legitimate tax-targets. They were, however, strictly speaking, profiteers of the liberation, not of the occupation itself.

There were other categories of profiteer, for example farmers "who during the first years of the occupation sold their produce at large prices." However, these "are said to have hoarded the proceeds which have since evaporated due to the inflation." At the end of the occupation, most were left with wretchedly depleted livestock and equipment inventories.[80] Contractors to the occupation forces could do relatively well for themselves, though most of their turnover would have been redistributed as wages and payments to suppliers. In any case this was a highly risky trade, because of the frequent payment stops which the Germans imposed. Till the end of 1942, large speculative profits could also be made by importers, who benefited from the absurd overvaluation of their drachmas, relative to the mark, and by Greek "students" in Vienna and elsewhere in the Reich, who could live high on the hog because of the enormous purchasing power of their drachma remittances when exchanged into marks at the official rate.[81]

In times when most people suffer hardship, those who can protect their resources become conspicuous, and the subject of acute envy. The amount of "new" money the occupation created was far less substantial than was imagined by public opinion. Not a few businesses were ruined too, by a requirement under a law of 1941, which severely restricted the ability of employers to lay off labour. The law was enacted by the Greek government of the occupation period in order "to demonstrate to the Germans that they had no unemployed, and consequently no surplus labour for export" to the Reich. As a result, employers "in many cases had to liquidate or disperse their assets." "Certain employers," it was alleged were "restrained from going into bankruptcy so long as they had any assets of any description left to realise." The problem was so acute that one of the earliest enactments of the liberation government, on 25 November 1944, was to soften (though not to abolish) the provisions of the law of 1941, as they applied to the private sector.[82] Economic life in occupied Greece was a roller coaster, for business no less than for labour. The endlessly repeated mantra that only businessmen benefited, and that all wage earners were driven to the depths of poverty, was clearly tendentious.

Chapter 5. Waley's stabilisation (November 1944)

In the political vacuum caused by the German retreat, concern lest the ELAS guerrilla army seize Athens caused the British hastily to land an expeditionary force, and to secure the return of Georgios Papandreou's Greek National Unity government in exile.[83] On October 16, with British forces solidly established in the capital, Harold Macmillan, then Minister Resident at AFHQ, Caserta, landed with elements of this government. Both in military and in civil terms, the liberation government was wholly dependent on British assistance. Although well disposed towards Britain, it resented this dependence just as its predecessors had resented their own dependence on the Germans. The British, for their part, entertained no high regard for most of their Greek colleagues, towards whom they adopted a patronising attitude. The potential for conflict was present from the start. It was never de-fused.

In the field of finance, Anglo-Greek wartime relations were never free of friction. As an inducement to their reluctant participation in World War 1, the British government had arranged to pay for Greece's internal military spending as well as her foreign supplies, with the result that she ended the war a creditor of Britain.[84] On the outbreak of the Italo-Greek campaign in 1940, the British volunteered whole hearted assistance and loans to cover military and other supplies imported from the sterling area. Once more, the question of covering Greek internal spending was raised. The Greek authorities demanded British subsidies for this internal spending, and proceeded to act on the assumption that such subsidies had already been granted. J. M. Keynes at the Treasury was further concerned at Greek demands for the ring-fencing of Greek export and shipping earnings from the ambit of war finance, and for top price charters and insurance for shipping services represented by Greece's "fine collection of old hulks". The "appetite on the part of the Greek financiers" associated with the Bank of Greece "grows by what it feeds on", he warned, and cautioned the Treasury not to be snared by the "financial racket" of which it was the intended victim.[85] His concerns were justified. Greece was granted some £46 million of British loans but as only part of this was expended during the fighting, the Greek government went into exile controlling £37.3 million of sterling credits.[86]

The British were provided with further advance notice of the probable predatory and feckless reaction of the Greek authorities towards them after the liberation. When Italy surrendered in September 1943, the British took Samos island from its Italian occupiers. They held it till forced by the Germans to evacuate in November. The islanders were delighted at the arrival of the British, but their liberation was disastrously mishandled. An excessively high drachma-sterling rate was fixed for troop pay, which was worsened by unremitting inflation. This deprived the British forces of spending power, and caused army supplies to appear on the street markets.[87] The Vathi branch of the Bank of Greece carried about 1 billion drachmas - enough to finance about three months administrative spending. The Greek Provisional Council, to whom the proceeds were turned over, along with food aid valued at 1,034 million drachmas, proceeded "on a programme of lavish spending." All factions competed for a share. The *andartes* - guerrillas - quickly grabbed 65 million drachmas. Those employed on the administrative payroll awarded themselves 150 percent pay rises. The food aid was supposed to be sold on ration but was largely given away, since only 122 million drachmas returned in revenue from it. 70 percent of the Bank of Greece's cash vanished within a month. "Samos found it could obtain abundant food supplies without parting with its precious olive oil." When the Council discussed a proposal to advance 30 million drachmas to "needy lawyers" the British realised, too late, the need for "a projected deflationary measure." However the local officials anticipated it by awarding themselves bonuses and increments. The army staff pointed out the obvious lessons for the future in the light of this experience of "subversive non-co-operation." It does not appear that the lesson was learned.[88]

Before the liberation, the exile government was already at loggerheads with the British over future financial policies. In the British official view, the Greeks exaggerated the economic destruction inflicted on their country, so as to maximise their claim on future allied assistance. The perverse effect was that the British discounted their needs.[89] On the whole economic issues ranked low among the exile Government's preoccupations, apart from the general aim of extracting as much assistance as possible. The Greeks strove to achieve two objectives, both contrary to British intentions. Firstly, Greece should not bear part of the burden of its liberation. Secondly the Allies should do nothing to threaten the prospective revenue the Greek government could procure by printing money. Throughout the exile period, authority in financial matters resided in Kyriakos Varvaressos, who had served since before the war as Governor of the Bank of Greece, and formally retained the post. It was to his advice and opinions that the British attached the greatest respect. However, mutual jealousies and his connexion with the pre-war Metaxas regime led to his exclusion from the first post-liberation government. This was probably at the insistence of the E.A.M. socialist wing politicians recently brought within it. The exile government therefore paid increasing attention to Athens university Professor Xenophon Zolotas. On the eve of liberation, it made him "co-governor" of the Bank, entrusting him with its de facto leadership. Varvaressos, nominally retaining his post, had to cool his heels in London.[90] These gentlemen held differing views on prospective financial management, for Varvaressos alone accepted that Greece would have to continue making sacrifices for the common cause, and run its finances accordingly. From the Whitehall perspective however, these differences were less apparent than their shared concern to extract the utmost of assistance from Britain. The conflict was rather a reflection of the manoeuvring between factions in the struggle for power.

The British authorities intended to finance their local spending by circulating £BMA (British Military Administration pounds) as an interim currency. Zolotas however wanted the Bank of Greece to control the means of payment. This would take the form of a gold-backed "liberation drachma". The British would have to buy these drachmas for their local spending at a fixed exchange rate, and credit the Greek government account in London with the proceeds.[91] By this device, the Greeks would set the real cost to the British of acquiring their currency, regardless of what the "liberation drachma" happened to be worth domestically. In the Greek view, the British military should live entirely on the supplies it brought in with it. The allied troops, when receiving their pay in liberation currency, should be instructed only to use it for "essential" needs.[92] Varvaressos did not want the army to introduce the £BMA, because he could not "obtain a satisfactory undertaking from His Majesty's Government on the question of the refund to the Greek Government in sterling of sums expended in BMA notes by forces in Greece."[93]

The existing hyperinflation in occupied Greece did not seem to present any future problem for the liberation era. It therefore gave rise to no preparatory planning. In the closing weeks of the German occupation, the London based Greek finance ministry expected that after the liberation, inflation would stop of its own accord. It anticipated an immediate fall in prices, which would "raise the purchasing power of the drachma."

The fall in prices, calculated via the Fisher monetary equation, would result from the prompt return of the velocity of circulation to normal.[94] The views here probably reflect those of Varvaressos.[95] This scenario was largely accepted by the British, who did not expect to inherit the inflation problem from the occupation regime. The Foreign Office concurred that "the liberation would restore confidence in the drachma, that there would be a substantial fall in prices and that at least a measure of stability would be achieved."[96] The British army, in a wrong-headed memorandum, thought likewise. It "attache[d] little importance to recent fantastic prices for sovereigns and goods in short supply," and expected a sharp fall in them.[97]

In view of the extremity of the currency collapse which had been caused by deficit financing, London assumed that the liberation government would forswear recourse to the printing press. The Greeks thought otherwise. According to the highly optimistic Greek scenario, the automatic self-stabilisation of the drachma would enable, indeed oblige, the authorities to replenish the extremely shrunken real money supply. This would secure them a cornucopia of non-fiscal revenue. Moreover, the spontaneous subsidence of drachma prices (they claimed) would enable them "to tax these inflationary profits."[98] This indicated their intention to utilise inflation itself as a base for taxing business, as their predecessors had tried to do during the occupation. The Greeks did not want the £BMA to circulate. They feared lest it "cause loss of confidence in Greek currency, while they were trying to build it up." In other words, circulation of the £BMA would lessen their own capacity to secure seigniorage without inflationary consequences.

The British Treasury was reluctant to give Varvaressos the assurances he sought on currency arrangements. It was annoyed by the unwillingness of the Greeks to contribute towards their own liberation. "I feel strongly" advised J R Trevaldwyn, "that we should remind [Varvaressos] once more that HMG have for five years borne the whole cost of the war in the Middle East; that they are now proposing to bear a substantial part of the cost of liberating Greece ... and that they trust that, in the circumstances, the Greek authorities will be able to accept our present proposals."[99] These proposals did not include letting the Greek government fix the rate of exchange between the drachma and the £BMA. The British military were determined to fix the rate themselves, and not to fall into the fixed exchange rate trap entered earlier by the Germans which had virtually wiped out the purchase power of their soldiers' pay in Greece. In practice £BMA were circulated by the military paymasters after the liberation. As the drachma was "for all practical purposes completely valueless," they let the £BMA float, anticipating that it would quickly displace the drachma from circulation.[100] This was exactly what the Greek government wanted to avoid.

The emergent conflicts of interests in the run-up to liberation foreshadowed much that followed. The British were mindful of the future fiscal difficulties of the Greek government, and tried to ease them. However, they did expected the Greeks to tax themselves heavily, and bear a share of the burden. Greece, however, expected most of its costs of government to be carried at somebody else's expense. It would pay its own bills by printing drachmas, secured, if possible, on British credit. The pre-liberation dispute between the Greeks and the British was never resolved.

On its arrival in Athens, the new Greek government was without current revenue sources, save for its control of the printing press. It was destitute even of the funds to establish a National Guard. It lacked the means or the will to re-establish an effective fiscal administration. It needed to keep the utilities running at government cost. Like the authorities on Samos the previous year, the new government wanted only to appease its citizens, by spreading the bounty of the printing presses as widely as possible. In the view of a visiting Treasury official, Sir David Waley, "the Greek government are in effect paying doles to a large part of the population who spend all day parading in the streets in idleness with political demonstrations as their chief occupation. This is Beveridge with a vengeance."[101] As a result, instead of abating, inflation exploded. There seemed to be no Greek plan for tackling the crisis. Nor did the Greek authorities show much interest in the topic. The British quickly became exasperated with Greek officials. "While outwardly very helpful, ... [they] seemed incapable of producing statistics or a co-ordinated wage policy." Even Zolotas, at the Bank of Greece, who had pinned his hopes on being given a supply of £BMA notes, "confessed he did not know what to do."[102] To keep all concerned happy, the government drove the note press even more energetically than its predecessor, believing that its credit enjoyed greater confidence. It extracted 304 million drachmas of 1940 in seigniorage in October and 357 million in November, compared with 214 million raised in September. As a result, inflation speeded up from

1,917 percent in August/September to 7,459 percent in September/October. Prices rose faster still in the early days of November.

These revenues would not have to be shared as formerly with an occupying power. However the British army was also putting £BMA into circulation, at the rate of around £782,000 BMA a month, or - in very rough terms for October and November - the equivalent of 120 million drachmas of 1940. When this money was withdrawn through exchange into drachmas, it would be credited to Greece's (blocked) sterling balance, but in the short run, its issue had precisely the same effect as an occupation levy, since it was un-linked with a corresponding inflow of merchandise. Therefore, the total purchasing power extracted in seigniorage after the liberation ran at around 420-480 million 1940 drachmas a month. So high a rate had not been sustained since 1943, when the real (drachma) money base had been about ten times larger.

The new government may have been correct in supposing that the liberation would restore confidence in the currency. Its capacity to create seigniorage at this rate depended on a greater residual willingness of the public in those areas where the drachma circulated to hold Greek money. By applying the Fisher equation, Makinen represents the "typical drachma note" to be held at this period for about 4 hours before being spent, i.e. to circulate 250 times as fast as in 1938. This is unrealistic, for fiat money appears to have supported few transactions outside the Athens area.[103] Even in Athens it competed in circulation not only with gold coins and £BMA, but also with commodity monies. For example, when the British liberated Athens, admission to the cinema cost a cake of soap, two packets of cigarettes - or 40 million drachmas.[104] It is therefore impossible to estimate the true circulation velocity of the drachma.

Since the British had regarded currency matters as lying ultimately within the purview of the Greek government, no advance guidance was provided to Macmillan on the control of inflation. Such was its intensity however, that he treated currency stabilisation as a matter of urgent priority. He warned Papandreou that his government would collapse unless it attended to the currency situation.[105] Macmillan was, of course, thinking in terms of fiscal reform. The Greek government and the Bank of Greece agreed they had a problem, but shied away from this solution. They had decided on one of their own. Three days after arriving in Athens they asked Macmillan for delivery - with the utmost urgency - of 200,000 gold sovereigns. These were to be sold on the Athens market to steady the drachma exchange rate. They considered this "the only practical method of arresting the price of the sovereign."[106] There is no evidence that they were consciously emulating Neubacher's "gold action" to sustain the yield of seigniorage on a permanently inflating currency. Still, if this was the inspiration they could hardly have admitted to it. Macmillan reckoned that "these [sovereigns] will just go down the drain in a few days,"[107] and ignored the request. However the Greek government cabled London for the equivalent in gold to be drawn from its gold reserve and the counterpart in sovereigns flown to Athens. The expeditionary force saw the plan as vital to securing stability, so the British War Office lent its backing. It advocated it as the only means by which the Greek government could make its "necessary payments," and recommended the "earliest and sympathetic consideration of this request."[108] Financial specialists thought otherwise. At the Treasury, under-secretary Sir David Waley reckoned the amount of money involved insufficient for stabilisation purposes. He predicted (accurately) that their sale would "worsen the situation when they were exhausted." Rather he called for heavy taxation, and in the interim, a scheme for the Greek government to borrow, presumably internally, on promises of repayment in gold.[109] The Governor of the Bank of England also told the Treasury he thought the sale of sovereigns was "a stupid plan, and likely to make the difficulties worse rather than better."[110] Nevertheless, Waley's judgement and his own were over-ridden, probably because of the security imperative. The Treasury decided that "if the Greek government was determined to waste its gold reserves, they would supply the 200,000 sovereigns." It did not however bother to inform the British administrators on the spot.[111]

Ignorant of this development, Macmillan convened his advisers to prepare their own stabilisation plan. They recommended issuing the £BMA as an interim Greek currency, and sent a representative to London to get the scheme sanctioned.[112] There was no immediate response, but an urgent message from Athens brought Foreign Secretary Anthony Eden out on the 25th. He cabled Churchill to send him "a first class treasury expert."[113] Consequently two Treasury knights arrived on the 30th, under-secretaries Sir David Waley, and Sir Louis Beale. Waley brought with him a hastily drafted memorandum, and Eden was given the gist of its contents.

Waley's aim, as he had stated earlier in Treasury, was to re-establish fiscal rectitude, towards which the Greeks were only prepared to pay lip-service. The government was to hack back its bloated pay-roll. There was plenty of scope, as government pay had widely been granted in the closing stages of the occupation as outdoor relief. The government was also to re-start collecting taxes. Given the paralysis of economic activity, and the widespread destitution, an early return to fiscal balance was hardly to be expected. Therefore the Greek treasury was encouraged to secure the greater part of its revenue from the sale of IRC relief rations. A new drachma currency was to be established to restore confidence. Recognising the inflationary danger of financing reconstruction by emitting new money after stabilisation, the authorities were also enjoined to start encouraging savings and to float internal loans.

Most important of all, as Waley impressed upon Macmillan, the system of wage calculation had to be altered.[114] Macmillan did not elaborate on this point, and there is no trace of Waley's original memorandum in British Treasury, Foreign Office or Bank of England files. Waley consistently demanded austerity. US ambassador Lincoln McVeagh, though he liked Waley personally, was convinced that he was "extremely poorly informed on Greece." By this he meant that Waley underestimated the living standard expectations of the Greeks.[115] To Waley, and to his British colleagues, wage determination was deemed a key issue, because of the alleged cost-push caused by wage setting procedures in the last few months of the occupation, which had so depleted business inventories. The British were adamant that Greece must abolish this automatic linkage of wages with the cost of living. Waley offered no guarantee that his plan would work. From the start he regarded it as a "highly risky affair," and later as an exercise in "achieving the impossible."

By the time of his arrival, the Greeks had secured the promise of the sovereigns for their gold sales programme. This at least offered some hope of achieving a short term stabilisation of prices, so Waley swallowed his earlier reservations, and assented to their urging of the plan. Since the supply already ordered would not suffice, he associated his own authority with a request by the Greek government for a further supply of sovereigns to be flown to Athens. He represented them as "a gold cushion" that might avert failure."[116] The Greeks asked for 500,000 sovereigns, but the British cynically reckoned they would be happy to settle for half that amount. The Treasury again assented, and despatched 250,000 sovereigns to Athens, against its better judgement.[117] However, a few days later Waley reported that the Greeks intended to postpone the stabilisation till January 1946. He agreed with the postponement, because "it would be hopeless to stabilise with so large a deficit," especially as there were as yet no budget plans worthy of the name. The sovereigns already ordered would be sold to hold the drachma rate more or less stable till the postponed stabilisation was carried out.[118] So government gold sales resumed at the beginning of November.[119] The "gold action" was therefore re-instated about three weeks after its cessation. It held the drachma exchange rate for a few days. This probably facilitated the issue of new money, but such was the pressure of the liberation government for funds that this transient stability was swiftly overwhelmed - as Waley had predicted.

The new "gold action" was only envisaged as preliminary to stabilisation (i.e. the tying of the drachma to some or other notionally stable standard). The Greek authorities seem really to have believed that this intervention could *de facto* end the inflation. Despite the obvious shortcomings of the scheme, and the casual way in which it was handled, it could, theoretically, have succeeded. It would certainly have been useful to have had a bigger intervention reserve on hand, but the market was not to know how large it was, only that it existed. The key to stopping a hyperinflation is to panic the market into believing the programme will work. If that is successful, the intervention fund need never be touched. The central bank will become a net buyer, not a seller, of hard currency. Neubacher (who in his memoirs envied the British the far greater resources they disposed for dealing with the Greek finances) had understood this clearly, and had played the markets on this principle. A bad defect of the sovereign sales scheme lay probably in the very secrecy with which the operation was carried out. The authorities failed to understand the guiding rule of stabilising a currency. It is the market which does the job, by adjusting its demand for transactions money, not the government, so secrecy is only likely to undermine the operation. The mind-set of administrators in a war environment was however so attuned to confidentiality that secrecy was an automatic rather than a considered response to the situation.

With the failure of this half-hearted stabilisation, the Greek government now feared civil disturbance, even civil war, if effective stabilisation were postponed till January. So despite Waley's extreme pessimism as to its likely success, the British stabilisation plan was reinstated.[120]

The British intended the Waley plan to be served by *diktat* on the

Greeks. Eden described it as "Dr. Waley's prescription for the patient," identifying the "patient" as Prime Minister Papandreou. On November 1, Waley presented his memorandum to Macmillan's committee of advisers. It "was accepted by everybody in principle."[121] Imagining that the Greeks would indeed accept the *diktat*, Eden departed on the eternal diplomatic round.

In fact, the *diktat* turned by degrees into a messy compromise. On November 3, Macmillan confronted Papandreou and pro-Communist finance minister Alexandros Svolos, to tell them they must implement the plan. He warned that they would receive no further British assistance until stabilisation had been carried out, and had been made to hold. Papandreou quickly agreed, though Svolos needed to be pressed hard for his assent.[122] This obstacle cleared, talks could begin at the Bank of Greece on the implementation of the plan.

The central issue on the British agenda was the balancing of the budget. This was not a Greek priority. Only on British pressing did Finance Under-secretary Angelos Angelopoulos (also an E.A.M. nominee) hastily draw up a budget. As government expenditure was largely composed of wage and salary payments, wage setting and employment levels became the key point of dispute. Angelopoulos' aggregate for government wages and salaries in the budget was set (in sterling terms) at some five times pre-war. This was absurd. In real terms his proposed government pay bill was a quarter or more higher than pre-war, but had to be financed from a drastically shrunken national income, much of which lay out of the reach of the government. The Greek side explained this as the cost of 20,000 "extra" employees who had been employed by the Germans. Finance also had to be provided for the public utility pay-roll, as the utilities were not apparently expected to generate any contribution to revenue.[123] These provisions, it was promised, were transient. (In fact they were not). At his meetings with the Greek authorities, Waley insisted on abolishing wage indexation, and on setting a wage scale which was to be frozen. The Greek side assented. Nevertheless it wanted to maximise wage rates because of political pressures to buy popular assent. This was why the budget had accommodated a government wage average at a relatively high nominal 10 shillings a day.

The British pounced on this ten shilling wage, which they regarded as unsustainable and "pressed hard for five shillings."[124] Faced with British condemnation of his budget as "completely unsatisfactory", Angelopoulos promptly offered to revise it. This casual back-down indicated, in Patterson's view, the "lack of seriousness on the part of the Greeks."[125] A revised budget draft was submitted three days later, in which draft expenditure was cut a little. Government salaries and pensions were now budgeted at an average seven shillings a day.[126] The British still objected. Waley declared his unchanged preference for a 5 shilling wage over the Greek compromise figure of 7 shillings.[127] However, he was challenged by Svolos, who argued that "as long as the rations distributed were insufficient, workers must be paid wages high enough to buy food on the open market". No agreement was reached so no formal wage tariff was published to accompany the stabilisation plan. Setting the wage tariff lay within the Greek sphere of competence, and Waley could only advise.

On the revenue side of the budget, most income was to come from the resale of relief supplies. £15 million (sterling) was budgeted in taxes but no indication was offered as to the basis on which it would be raised. Still, the British felt "this was as good a budget as was possible under the circumstances,"[128] and accepted it as an element in the stabilisation plan.

The Greeks put forward their own agenda at the talks. They knew the budget was mere window dressing, and that spending would far exceed revenue. Therefore they were most concerned not to renounce their right to print money. Zolotas, now in charge at the Bank of Greece, proposed that once the new drachma was issued, the old drachma should be kept in circulation without pegging its parity to the new. Ostensibly, this would promote confidence in the new currency by divorcing it from the old.[129] The device was really to protect the new drachma "if the state was unable in the first period to cover its expenditure fully and was therefore forced to have recourse to a greater extent to the printing machine." Zolotas "felt no certainty that the government would not ask the Bank of Greece to print as many notes after stabilisation as before." In that case he preferred to safeguard the new currency and continue inflationary note issuing in old drachmas.[130] This would cause the gold value of the old drachma to continue falling, but as issue of the new drachma would be strictly controlled, it would not be similarly affected. The risk of a "more intense flight from the old drachma" could be stopped by supporting its exchange rate with gold.[131]

Zolotas cited the Soviet experience of 1923/4 with the dual circulation of the paper *sovznak* and the (nominally) gold-backed *chervonets*. The *chervonets* had been a large, strictly indivisible unit, worth about £1. Consequently most retail transactions had to be conducted in inflationary *sovznaks*, and the issue of *sovznaks* provided the Soviet authorities with deficit finance without destabilising the *chervonets*.[132] However, the stream of *sovznaks* that poured from the Soviet printing presses caused them to lose value at hyperinflationary speed. So Zolotas needed to explain why anybody, given a free choice between the new and old currencies, would accept payment in the old, especially as tax payments would have to be made in the new currency. The most likely explanation is that Zolotas had planned to repeat the Soviet experiment in detail. This would explain why, when proposing the creation of the "liberation drachma," the Greeks had in mind a unit equal in value to the pound:[133] they planned to use it as an indivisible Greek *chervonets*. Small everyday transactions would have to be carried out in old drachmas.

Zolotas did not press his scheme because he favoured the continued resort to deficit financing, rather because he doubted the ability of the Greek treasury to balance its accounts. He and Georgios Mantzavinos (then National Bank governor) were alleged, after the stabilisation, to have entered a mutual resignation pact, if the government drew on its credit with the Bank of Greece beyond a fixed limit.[134] On the other hand, his scheme was not mere insurance against an unintended budget over-shoot. He specifically advocated the use of old drachmas for non-wage administrative expenses, especially for payments in areas such as Crete, where inflation had been more moderate than in Athens, and where the population retained residual confidence in the old currency.[135]

Waley firmly quashed Zolotas' proposal to let the old drachma float, dismissing it as "based on a misunderstanding." (It is less clear who misunderstood whom). He reiterated his demand for the budget to be balanced. In opposing Zolotas, he was backed by his treasury colleague Beale, who "found the new co-governor Zolotos [sic] rather theoretical."[136] In the short run, the British insisted that the budget should be strengthened by limiting wage expenditures rather than by waiting for revenues.[137] The "old" drachma would become a fixed sub-multiple of the new, and therefore not an independent vehicle for extracting seigniorage.

Zolotas was a fiscal conservative compared with the Greek treasury ministers. They took a still more cavalier attitude to their financial problems, and tried to undermine his restraining influence. At the last of the four meetings which hammered out the stabilisation plan, Waley queried an article which had popped up in the draft stabilisation law. It stated that "the plus value of the cover as at 11 November 1944 constitutes a revenue of the state, to which it will pass." It transpired that Zolotas had been called away, and that Svolos had taken advantage of his absence to insert this clause. This effectively transferred the entire external reserve of the Bank of Greece to the Greek treasury. Zolotas naturally objected, and Waley forced Svolos to withdraw the article.[138]

Though Zolotas capitulated on the dual currency issue, the authorities continued surreptitiously to put old drachmas into circulation after the stabilisation. Indeed, in the first three days of the stabilisation, the circulation of old drachmas rose by 14.2 million new drachmas equivalent (£24,000).[139] The capacity of this back-door source of seigniorage was limited by the trivial value of the highest denominated old drachma note - 100 billion drachmas or 0.8 of a penny (sterling) at the official rate, for to print higher denominations which had not existed prior to stabilisation would have given the game away. Even so, in the next few months they issued "old" notes with a fixed-exchange value of about £200,000,[140] which no doubt provided somebody with a handy little slush fund.[141]

The "misunderstanding" to which Waley alluded, that is to say the conflict between the Greek desire to manage the currency as a seigniorage machine, and the British demand for fiscal stability, would persist throughout the whole lengthy episode of Greece's financial stabilisation and beyond it. Ultimately, to the Greek authorities, the finances of government were an instrument for buying loyalties and repressing independent interests. If that left a financial deficit, then the government could accuse its allies of insufficient generosity, and pressure them to boost the flow of aid.

The Waley plan called for the drachma to be called in and re-denominated at 50,000 million to 1. The new drachma was given limited convertibility to the £BMA at 600 to 1. £3 million BMA was made available to the Greek government to secure the currency, though perversely, this was to remain a secret. Implementation was carried out by the Greek authorities on 11 November 1944. (Greek sources refer to this as the "Svolos" stabilisation, though his input to it was minimal, and largely obstructive).

Waley's original plans for stabilisation, though hastily formulated, had been soundly based from a theoretical stand-point. Still, they took insufficient account of the political facts of post-liberation Greece. Waley was quickly to become aware of this. After Svolos' attempt to hi-jack the reserves of the Bank of Greece, Waley could be forgiven for seeing "no chance whatever" that recourse to the printing press to cover budget expenditure would stop.[142] He left Greece expressing the view that the drachma could be stabilised successfully if the government fixed wages at a "reasonable" level, restricted its own expenditure, and imposed adequate taxation - ensuring also that "those consumers who are not destitute" should pay adequately high prices for relief supplies.[143] He was however pessimistic as to the outcome, despite Papandreou's undertakings to Macmillan. Waley doubted whether the Greek ministers really understood the necessity to carry the programme out. He appraised from "their personal characters" and the government's internal difficulties that they would not risk implementing necessary but unpopular measures. "We are providing the supplies," he concluded. "The Greeks have plenty of brains: we cannot supply them with guts."[144]

The dispute over wage setting continued after the stabilisation. Rex Leeper, British Ambassador, told Svolos the seven shilling average was "dangerously high," but failed to convince him.[145] To force the issue, Angelopoulos leaked the proposed 7 shilling scale to the press in advance of agreement.[146] Svolos told Waley that "seven shillings represented a very substantial reduction." Waley countered that there could be no benefit to workers in increasing the supply of money independently of the supply of goods.[147] The outcome was the publication both of government and private employees' wage scales which were higher than the British had expected. As the Treasury was informed by the Foreign Office, "we find too that Angelopoulos double crossed us over government salaries which appear to be in excess of the agreed average."[148]

Not only was proposed government pay too high in the British view, the payroll itself was far too large. Initially, the E.A.M. ministers opposed redundancies, but a government consensus formed for the sacking of all civil servants who had been recruited under the Metaxas dictatorship and the occupation, and the cancelling of all promotions made over those nine years. So, to defend their jobs, younger civil servants joined E.A.M. en masse. Though the redundancy law was signed on 10 November, it remained a dead letter.[149]

Given the acute political uncertainties of the time, the lack of good faith with which the Greek authorities implemented the stabilisation, and the haste with which it was carried out, its effectiveness has been questioned. In the short term, it decelerated but failed to stop the hyperinflation. Price movements can be tracked from a new daily Bank of Greece index for locally procured goods. This was set at 100 on November 11, and rose by 2 December to 172.[150] The renewed inflation also dragged the price of the sovereign up, so much so that on the 21st Zolotas initiated a new "gold action" to support the currency.[151] It more or less held this exchange rate stable till the end of the month, and helped to damp the more general advance of prices, which had surged massively between the 15th and the 21st. These movements are shown in figure 5 (*i*) (see p. 66).

The continued inflation, and lack of confidence in the drachma can to some extent be ascribed to fear of a future armed conflict between the liberation government and ELAS, which would certainly have encouraged goods and gold hoarding. Of more significance, the high level of wages and low ration prices created shortages. (The budgetary effect of high wages would not yet have been disequilibriating). Skilled male labour drew 307 drachmas a day after 11 November, unskilled female 154,[152] (in sterling at the official parity, 10s 3d and 5s 2d). Bread rations of 125 drams per head per day were distributed at 50 lepta till the 18th, when the price was raised to 1 drachma (less than a halfpenny).[153] So the pressure on the exiguous supply of local goods was probably unsustainable.

On 3 December, the long-feared political showdown between ELAS and the British backed liberation government broke out. The Battle of Athens began with a mass demonstration as the cover for a pre-emptive coup by the ELAS guerrillas. They already surrounded the city, and now tried to seize control of it, before the government disposed sufficient force to counter them. Several weeks of desperate fighting followed. British forces, initially confined to a small area in the city centre, hung on till they could be reinforced. Then they gradually won the upper hand and expelled ELAS from the city.

Financial data for this period is understandably hazy, for the Athens banks were closed. According to Agapitides' index, the December aver-

Figure 5 (i)

Price movements following the 11 November 1944 stabilization

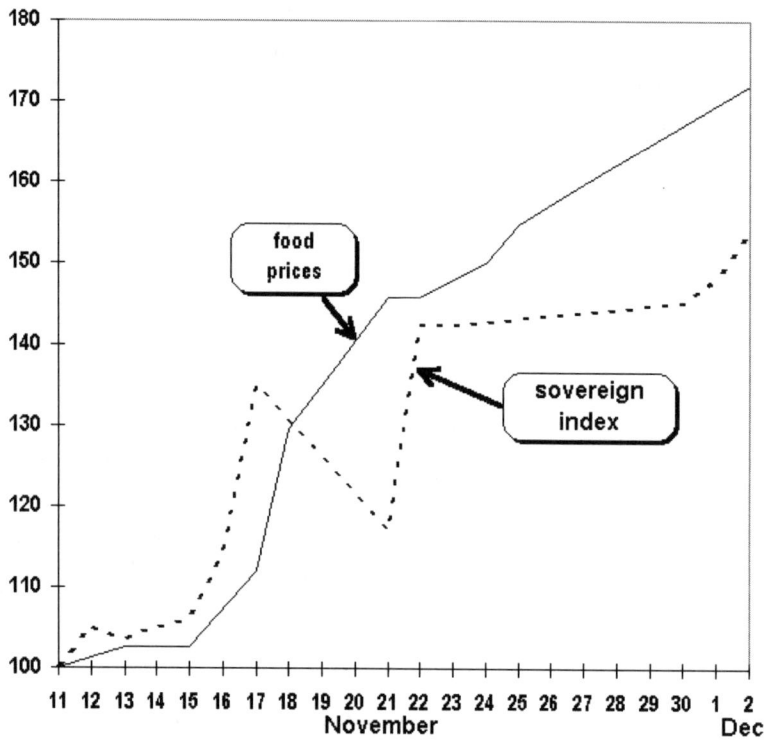

Sources: PRO FO 371 43725. Dispatches of 14 Nov., (fo. 5) 17 Nov. (fo. 37) 21 Nov. (fo. 59) 22 Nov. (fo. 134) 27 Nov. (fo. 183) 28 Nov., 3 Dec. (fo. 242.)

age of the Athens price level stood at 390, jumping from 172 at the beginning of the month. His data look plausible. The drachma weakened against gold. On 2 December the Athens gold price was 3,080 drachmas. At mid month on Patras and Salonica, it rose to 4,300, dragging up consumer prices there by 16 percent "in less than a week."[154] In Athens, British sources could not get details of essentials prices, but noted that they had soared to "fantastically high levels," because relief supplies were not getting through. Athens business was virtually shut down.[155] This price rise was driven solely by the breakdown in goods supply. Only a negligible amount of new money was emitted in December (53 million 1940 drachmas). This was unintentional. The vault of the Bank of Greece remained closed because one of the keys was held in ELAS territory. A fresh consignment of notes from London could not safely be off-loaded from the docks.[156]

By the end of December, ELAS forces had been cleared from Athens, and were being pursued into the rural areas. By mid-January, it was clear that ELAS had suffered a crushing defeat. In February, it settled for a highly disadvantageous peace (the Varkiza agreement). This enabled the Greek National Guard to extend its control to most other cities, and to dominate the Pelopponese. For several months, ELAS remained impotent to affect the course of events, though it was to regroup, and to consolidate its control in the north of Greece. Relief supplies, which could not be distributed during the worst of the fighting in Athens, were resumed. Security improved dramatically in most rural areas, and the peasants felt confident enough to resume cultivation.[157] Prices now fell rapidly.

To survey the Greek monetary experience over the stabilisation and post stabilisation period, we have recourse to our series for real M1. The data are displayed in table A5 and results displayed as figure 8. (i) (see p. 102). The money supply consisted of new Bank of Greece notes, and "old" drachmas still in circulation, all at mid month, and deflated by the rent excluded cost of living at the November and the December average. Bank deposits (for which no data were published) seem to have been negligible. The figures show the following trend. Confidence improved in November, with real balances 203 percent of the October average, but real drachma money supply per person rose from a microscopic 4.2 drachmas of 1940 per head to a still trivial 8.7. Obviously when working with the precarious statistical base for this period, such quantitative statements cannot be taken as definitive. Still, is clear from the supporting evidence that the stabilisation arrested the speed of inflation, and the complaints that merchants were refusing to sell for drachmas cease. The fig leaf of £BMA convertibility impressed nobody, for the Greeks had hard experience of military currencies that ended up worthless. After the stabilisation, the public began dumping £BMA on the Bank of Greece, to acquire drachmas.[158]

Because of the modest rise in the transactions demand for drachmas, government managed to reap more in seigniorage in November than in October (605 million drachmas of 1940 value against 304 million in October.) This evidence signals a boost to confidence in the drachma, albeit tentative. In December on the other hand, warfare caused an involuntary monetary squeeze, because of the extreme shortage of accessible notes in government hands. Yet real per capita balances advanced a further 73 percent in December to 15.1 drachmas of 1940. For January, with ELAS heading for defeat, monetary changes have been estimated indirectly. By linking Agapitides' index (which ends in December 1944) with the new Bank of Greece indexes which link stabilisation day prices to those of January, but record no figure for December, we estimate that in January prices fell by 45.6 percent from their December level. Consequently confidence in the drachma revived. The real (fiat) money supply per head recovered in January from 15.1 drachmas of 1940 in December to 53.6 drachmas. Prices fell by a further 15.6 percent in February, and the money supply rose to 129 drachmas.

Clearly it was the defeat of ELAS and the return of cheap relief food that helped inflation expectations to reverse so dramatically. The return of public confidence in the drachma was far stronger than had been secured in November by that month's stabilisation. Yet on this occasion, no new financial measures were taken to boost confidence in the drachma. Rather the contrary. The Bank of England told Zolotas at the Bank of Greece (Waley concurring) that the policy of supporting the drachma on the market with sovereigns had been mistaken.[159] Thereupon, under British pressure, he ceased to sell gold.[160] An additional stabilising influence was that inflation had lowered real wages by 53 percent from their November level.[161]

This sequence of events enables us to set the outcome of the 11 November monetary reform in its true perspective. Its very tentative initial results cannot be attributed to its intrinsic defect, the lack of government seriousness over the need for financial discipline which so worried Waley. This was not public information. The success of programmes for stabilisation from hyperinflation depends on engineering a reversal of inflation expectations on the part of the public, such as the liberation government had earlier vainly hoped would happen spontaneously. If the public expects an end to inflation, or a significant drop in the inflation rate it will release inventories and rebuild its cash balances, awarding the state the capacity to carry on deficit spending, for a limited period and on a one-time basis.

At this point the reform may be merely cosmetic. Makinen argues reasonably that the November reform was indeed "little more than a cosmetic change." However, the public was not as yet in a position to appraise the determination of the authorities to end inflation in the longer term. The reform was also poorly publicised. Makinen even claims that it "was probably not much less of a surprise to the government than it was to the Greeks."[162] This is a slight exaggeration, for the forthcoming currency reform was publicly announced on 9 November.[163] In fact, prices peaked that day, and immediately began to fall back,[164] which indicates a reversal of market expectations. On stabilisation day, the Athens press carried a detailed statement of the new parities, a forecast of improved relief supplies, and an (insincere) announcement that the budget would be balanced. With this objective, a heavy new war profits tax was to be applied immediately.[165] However, the reform was executed in a hasty muddle. Only two new notes were released,[166] the larger of which, for a mere 50 drachmas, (1s 8d) carried the date of January 1941 rather than November 1944. Few of these notes came quickly into circulation, for on stabilisation day a mere 25 million new drachmas were issued (compared with 128 million in old).[167] Rather than reform their finances it appears that the authorities continued to pursue their former practice of issuing money day by day to meet their bills. It was "pay as you print".

The secrecy surrounding the £BMA convertibility arrangements also did little to enhance confidence. Even the recovery of confidence in November was very tentative. But with allowance for all this, the attempt by ELAS to seize control and expel the British was (as Karatzas argues) widely expected. Its most probable outcome, an ELAS victory, did not inspire confidence in the currency. So distrust of the new drachma after the November reform may have reflected a depth of political pessimism that eclipsed other considerations.

In the existing literature there is confusion about the effectiveness of the November reform and the return of confidence, mainly because of the ambiguity of the statistical sources. Cagan represented the Waley reform as reversing short-term inflation expectations, and ignored the still violent inflation of late November and December. A table constructed by Makinen shows a fall in the "real note index" (circulation deflated by the gold price) in November which was more than reversed by a strong rise in December.[168] Karatzas queried why the public should have recovered any faith in the drachma, that is to say, why it should have been prepared sharply to increase its real balances in drachmas in the midst of a "full scale bloody civil war."[169]. He suggested that there had to be something amiss with Makinen's calculations. In his response, Makinen suggested that the "decisive British intervention," in that war "might well have bolstered confidence."[170] During the Battle of Athens, rising confidence in the drachma, as measured by real M1, would have to turn on the positive expectations instanced by Makinen in his rebuttal to Karatzas; but for the public to have managed sharply to raise its real money holdings at this time really is straining credulity.

This point of dispute rose essentially through the use of monthly averages of real transactions balances during a period of rapid and violent short term fluctuations. By breaking the period from November 1944 - January 1945 into shorter segments, as in table 5.1, we can show what actually happened.

This puts the changes into a clearer perspective. Till the 11 November reform the real circulation remained minuscule, but it then rose strongly till the end of the month. In December, the Battle of Athens cut it back by half (because of the acute shortage of commodities) but it rebounded massively in January.

Let us compare the adjustment impact with that of Neubacher's "October Miracle" in 1942. In October 1942, the supply of fiat money per person (in terms of 1940 purchasing power) rose from 192.4 drachmas to 279.3 in November and 450.5 in December. In 1944, the corresponding monthly figures were 4.2, 8.7 and 15.1 (1940) drachmas. So confidence in the currency, though rising sharply, remained at an incredibly low level compared even with 1942, to say nothing of 1940 when the money supply provided around 3,744 drachmas per head. The weakness of confidence is particularly striking if we consider the heavy sales of

Table 5.1. Money supply around the November 1944 stabilisation.

	note issue (old drachmas)	prices 1940=1	real M1 1940 dr.
October '45	7.3×10^{17}	2.361×10^{9}	31 m
11 November	7.6×10^{18}	2.035×10^{11}	37 m
30 November	6.8×10^{19}	3.375×10^{11}	201 m
December	8.7×10^{19}	7.931×10^{11}	109 m
January '46	1.7×10^{20}	4.311×10^{11}	387 m

Sources and calculation: for October, December and January, see table A5. For 11 and 30 Nov. circulation figures see B of E OV 80 22. fo. 145; PRO FO 371 43726. fo. 136. For prices 11 Nov. see table A5 (end). Prices for local commodities, where 11 November = 100, on 27 Nov. and 2 Dec. were 159.9 and 172. PRO 371 43725, Leeper 28 Nov. 1944, and fo. 242.

gold with which the drachma was supported by the authorities at the beginning of November and in the initial weeks of the stabilisation.[171]

The sequence of events thus far makes it largely irrelevant as to whether or not the November 11 stabilisation was "cosmetic". By labelling it as such, Makinen and associates are exercising hindsight concerning the (non) implementation of the Waley measures which was not possible to the Greek public at the time. Political expectations eclipsed such niceties, the all important question was whether or not Greece would go Communist and expel the British. It was only after this issue was settled (for the time being) that the health of the drachma would come to depend on the prospective conduct of fiscal policy. In the meantime, there was still plenty of scope for taxation by seigniorage.

Thus stabilisation really became effective only from January 1945, buying the authorities a few months during which real money balances rose sharply - long enough for them to re-order their finances and end dependence on the printing press. They did nothing of the kind. The composition of the new administration headed by General Nikolaos Plastiras shifted right-wards, but proved no more earnest than its predecessor in carrying out the fiscal obligations undertaken to Macmillan.

During the discussions which preceded the November stabilisation, concern by the British over the budget had focused mainly on expenditure. They assumed that the resale of relief supplies would provide Greece with a revenue base for frugal government, till ordinary tax revenues were normalised. This assumption proved disastrously inaccurate. After the liberation, Herculean efforts were made to provide Greece with relief deliveries, mainly of foodstuffs. These deliveries were initially handled by (British) Military Liaison, after which responsibility was transferred to UNRRA. The value of this aid, as administered by UNRRA between April and December 1945, amounted to $350 million - or about half the net pre-war national income of Greece, according to Makinen.[172] Yet between November 1944 and June 1945, relief food distributions furnished no net revenue after the deduction of distribution costs.[173] Seeking to exonerate the Greek authorities for this shortfall, Karatzas attributes it to the objections of the donors to the resale of aid deliveries.[174] This matter had indeed caused momentary difficulties with the American and Swedish donors who wanted the aid to be distributed gratis, but their objections were over-ridden by Macmillan.[175] UNRRA also wanted to confine subsidies on the distribution of bread to the poor,[176] but the Greek government insisted on setting a minimal universal distribution price, creating a flourishing black market in the resale of relief grain.[177] Revenues covered but 6.5 percent of spending as late as February 1945.

Expenditure did not meet with expectations either. In 1940 drachmas, government expenditures passing through the Bank of Greece rose from 212 million in January to 377 million in February and 819 million in March. The Angelopoulos budget had allowed only £2.62 million (sterling) for a year's military expenditure,[178] presumably since the left had no desire to strengthen the National Guard vis-à-vis the guerrillas. After the Battle of Athens, military spending soared. The British estimated it would soon approach a billion drachmas (£1.6 million sterling) a month.[179]

Pay setting also got out of hand. The concessions the Greeks had made on pay rates when setting the budget were voided by fixing basic unskilled day wage rates at 192 drachmas, skilled 307 drachmas[180] (6s 5d - 10s 3d). At 192 drachmas, unskilled wages compared with 60 drachmas a day pre-war, that is to say they were set close to their real-terms parity with pre-war, because the rent inclusive cost of living, computed in new drachmas at stabilisation, was 3.8 times pre-war.[181] Higher grades fared less well but these rates were excessive in relation to Greece's shrunken productive capacity. Liberal finance minister Georgios Sideris acquired a reputation as "a champion of labour,"[182] and although prices continued to fall heavily from January through March, government employees were given a hefty wage increase of 53 percent in March, which immediately fed through to budget spending.

The British became increasingly uneasy because of lack of effort by Sideris to return to sound money. Waley revisited Athens in early February in a vain attempt to put pressure on him. Sideris' Liberal Party drew heavily on the business vote,[183] so he could not be pressed to institute a retrospective tax on war profiteers. He also quickly withdrew a half hearted effort to raise relief goods prices in the face of protest.[184] Patterson represents Sideris and his colleagues as overwhelmed by the impossibility of their task, but Sideris lost little sleep on account of the nation's financial problems. He saw his main task as to press the British for a large loan which would absolve the Greeks from the need to tax themselves.[185] As none was forthcoming, he cordially resented British interference. He complained that "he was always being asked whether he proposed to follow an orthodox fiscal policy," and to maintain the drachma exchange rate, "as if there could be much point in his doing so ... if the rest of the national economy subsided in ruins all around it."[186] Consequently British officials regarded him as a "tough and misguided creature."[187]

The only senior Greek administrator to worry about the fiscal imbalance was Varvaressos, who returned to Athens from London at the end of January to assume once more his post of Governor of the Bank of Greece. (Zolotas returned for the time being to academic life.) On 30 January, he commented to the British that "Greece was living beyond her means." The size of the army and level of pay rates were excessive, and should "correspond to economic conditions."[188] Shortly afterwards, Eden "spoke very frankly" to Sideris,[189] and demanded "resolute" anti-inflationary measures. He advised cutting military pay by 75 percent, both because of the budgetary strain it imposed, and because of the demand pressures high pay rates imposed upon an inelastic supply of consumers goods. The Greeks ignored these admonitions, because General Plastiras would tolerate no curtailment of his army's prerogatives.[190]

Despite the continued fall in prices, the key black market exchange rates on the dollar and the sovereign sagged from January onward. These rates were highly volatile despite drachma "convertibility" with the £BMA. The £BMA was itself not exportable and not convertible to sterling, though the Greek public was not supposed to know that.[191] It had been arranged that the £BMA notes would be redeemed by the Greek central bank within 12 months by payment in drachmas. The return of these notes to Britain would be credited to Greece's blocked sterling account. So as £BMA convertibility was the exclusive preserve of the Greek authorities, it was effectively tied to the drachma and not the other way round. Indeed, it was treated by Greeks, with bitter experience of military scrip, as even less desirable to hold, and most £BMA notes quickly found their way back to the central bank. Quoted in Athens at £BMA 5.1 to the sovereign on 24 November, it had sunk in value to 7.66 by 3 March 1945, and 20.83 by 2 May, though from March onward "real" sterling notes were exchanged for sovereigns at 7 to 1.[192] Embarrassed by the Greek government's debauching of their military currency, the British announced in April that they would in future buy drachmas at the Bank of Greece, and that the £BMA was to be withdrawn.[193]

Waley's recommendation that the government should eliminate its own deficits, partly so that savings deposits should flow into the banking sector to finance economic recovery was also ignored. Most new credits extended by the Bank of Greece were mopped up by budget spending. The Bank was unable to pass much new credit on through the banking system, and much of the credit it did extend was used, not to finance the economy, but to meet the banks' own pay-rolls.[194] Bank rate was pitched in February 1945 at 7 percent[195] so business was "insensitive to the cost of credit." Conversely, this implied such derisory returns on deposits that to lend money through legal channels was to invite speedy expropriation. So the real value of sight deposits of the banks in 1945 averaged 0.6 percent of 1938 and remained at derisory levels for several more years.[196] Savings were held in gold and in accumulated inventories, as the only inflation resistant media available. Demand for commercial credit (as well as treasury deficits) had to be satisfied by new money creation, and credit demand contained by rationing.[197]

The gains from the post-stabilisation adjustment of transactions balances could hardly last indefinitely, as successive governments failed to introduce order into the desperate financial situation. Sideris gained no credit for raising the price of relief supplies to reduce the Budget deficit, because the left wanted a full blooded effort at taxing "war profiteers" instead (i.e. taxing Sideris' party's own political supporters) and his refusal led to his replacement by Alexandros Mylonas (Agrarian) at the beginning of April.

The attack on Sideris was however a side show in a campaign, energetically supported by ambassador Leeper, to topple General Plastiras, the Prime Minister. Plastiras regarded the Varkiza agreement with ELAS as a betrayal and wanted to renew action against it. The British still hoped to bring ELAS back into the system of government, and wanted to avoid damaging their relations with the Soviets. So Plastiras had to go. The cover story was a contrived political scandal. The government fell on 4 April, and was replaced by a "service" government headed by Admiral Petros Voulgaris.[198] His new finance minister was Georgios Mantzavinos, former deputy to Varvaressos at the Bank of Greece. Patterson recalls him as an honourable man and sound on inflation, but as a minister, the British did not regard Mantzavinos as much of an improvement on Sideris. (Mylonas was only in office for a few days). He was described by them as an indecisive figure, happy only in Varvaressos' shadow, and events were to justify this view.[199]

Revenues rose, according to Makinen, to slightly over half of expenditure by May, but as half of them were secured from the resale of relief deliveries, which cost as much to distribute as they yielded, the budget remained hopelessly unbalanced.[200] Fiscal apathy for a time seemed to be justified by the ease with which seigniorage continued to be extracted from the new currency. However, the continued weakening of confidence in the currency was reflected by the climbing drachma-sovereign rate, followed by renewed high inflation, of 33.2 percent in April and 39.8 percent in May. Public expectations reversed accordingly, with a scramble out of fiat money and into goods and gold.

By May the exchange rate on the gold sovereign had soared to 19,000 drachmas and growth in the real money supply abruptly ceased. This signalled that the market could no longer absorb the current rate of new emissions of money. The pretence at implementing the Waley reform was dead. Policies simply had to change.

Chapter 6. The Third "End": The Varvaressos Reform (June 1945)

It was the British, not the Greeks, who wanted the urgent action. They brought sustained pressures to bear on the Voulgaris government. Mantzavinos had to present a balanced budget in May. Any fool can make the government accounts appear to balance ex-ante. The real test is to put up revenue and expenditure figures which are likely to balance ex-post, and in British eyes, "the whole thing [was] bogus."

Projected revenue amounted to 51.1 billion drachmas. Of this, some 23.7 billion was to come from the proceeds of relief supply sales, import duties and state monopoly receipts. The British thought these items unlikely to yield more than 18 billion, and no allowance was made on the expenditure side for the high cost of raising this revenue. A (nominally) important new measure, slated to raise 15 billion drachmas, was a retrospective tax on war profits, to punish "those who enriched themselves during the period of occupation." "Enrichment" embraced contracts with occupation forces, investments and gold purchases. The last of these had been a defensive activity essential for the protection of existing asset values, but was regarded of course as "speculation" and therefore culpable. The tax was imposed progressively, at rates ranging from 30 percent to 90 percent. It proved a wash-out. Between May and July it raised only 100 million drachmas.[201] Haphazard assessment procedures led to protracted appeals and although the tax was to yield 9.3 billion drachmas during the 1945/46 fiscal year, all but 2.7 billion were collected in 1946,[202] when the price level was 17 times higher than on budget day. Overall, the British were themselves optimistic in estimating that gross revenue would fall short of expectation by "at least 10 billion drachmas". Failure to allow for aid distribution costs, or to cost in subsidies for a new unemployment fund, caused expenditure to be underestimated by at least 8.5 billion drachmas, so about 44 percent of anticipated expenditure would remain uncovered by normal revenue.

The deficit could have been narrowed by pay-roll taxation. The pre-war withholding tax on government wages and salaries, which had vanished during the war, was to be reinstated, but at a mere 1 percent, which would barely exceed its collection cost. The British wanted it set at 20 percent - both to get revenue, and to offset the inflationary excess purchasing power "amongst the labouring classes." Mantzavinos was adamant in rejecting their recommendation. "The tax is not worth a general strike which would certainly follow if anything above 1 percent is proposed," he argued, and would bring about the fall of the government.[203] The British were half convinced - feeling that "we could not press the Greeks further on this point," for fear of civil disorders. Lamely, they settled "for control of prices and supplies, which alone could stop mounting prices and wages."[204]

Concerned at Mantzavinos' ineffectuality, the British increased the pressure on the Voulgaris government for a renewed fiscal reform. They did not conceal their preference for Varvaressos as their candidate for reformer. Keynes regarded that "very able old chap" Varvaressos so highly that he had wanted Greece given a seat on the drafting committee for the Bretton Woods conference, solely to bring Varvaressos in. (No Varvaressos, no seat for Greece).[205] Indeed he was widely regarded abroad as "perhaps the ablest post-war Greek official in Greek politics."[206] Nobody else, reckoned ambassador Rex Leeper "could save the situation."[207] Greek contacts could hardly speak too highly of him. He knew that tough measures to close the fiscal gap could no longer be side-stepped, and that he would have to design a far more convincing budget than his predecessors.

However, he also espoused a fierce egalitarianism. His aim was to combine fiscal discipline with a redistributive economic stabilisation and recovery, from whose benefits capitalist endeavour would be excluded. The philosophy underlying the reforms of his short but hectic tenure of special powers was foreshadowed in a memorandum to the British Treasury in April 1945. "The margin created by cancellation of the currency [i.e. the November stabilisation] has already been exhausted," he wrote. The situation had become "explosive," and "the increase" could not continue "at its present rate." Wage and salary levels had been kept at a "bare subsistence level." This affected work incentives, but goods supplies were unavailable to increase pay without risking renewed inflation. (This paved the way for a demand for more imports). So "a sharp fall in the prices of necessities" was the only way out of the country's difficulties.

At this stage he put forward no specific tax proposals. Rather he aired his concern with the past and present activities of the emergent "class of profiteers and collaborators with high purchasing power...." The new rich were able to appropriate the small quantities of local goods available and live in real comfort. He contrasted their lot with that of the workers and employees, whom it would be "difficult to persuade that [they] must still make all the sacrifices." His preferred "solution" was "heavy taxation on the rich." He offered no suggestion as to how their incomes should be taxed because the tax collecting machinery no longer existed, and because the class he wanted to hit was skilled in evasion.[208] A month later, he repeated his concern over the "surplus purchasing power held by ... the speculators, merchants or traders." So he told Treasury officials he was "thinking in terms of an arbitrary assessment on these gentry based on their outward and visible standard of life whether this be on the rents they are paying or on some other yardstick."[209] These points were to be subsumed into his programme.

Varvaressos was a complex figure, whose philosophy and political stance make tidy characterisation difficult. They were essentially consistent over time but were overlaid by tactical adjustments forced by changing circumstances. On the one hand, he was a consistent advocate of monetary stability - he was after all a central banker. Yet this was a means to an end which was not obviously compatible. "Monetary instability is in my view the greatest enemy of the poorer classes," he wrote in 1952. The improvement of their condition was "a desire ... which corresponds to my own feeling about the direction which the country's economic policy should take."[210]

His bete-noir, the "new bourgeoisie," he regarded as "a new economic oligarchy devoid of principles."[211] It consumed too much, and evaded the payment of its "fair share of the burden of government." Moreover, he was also convinced that businessmen liked monetary instability, because it enhanced their speculative profits. They took excessive margins, and speculated on inventories. Speculation was the source of the economic ills of Greece. To stabilise the economy, they had to be punished. His conviction that businessmen favoured financial instability (on which they could speculate) rested on the most fragile foundations. It flew in the face of such confidence indicators as the free market price of the drachma, the level of bank deposits, or of investment expectations, which consistently showed an extreme pessimism on profit expectations when instability worsened, and a revival of (qualified) optimism when it diminished. By his own logic however, his antipathy towards business predisposed him towards securing price stability, not through market forces, but through controls which would prevent "speculative" profits from being made.

In his opinion of business and businessmen, he shared the consensus of the Greek political establishment. He was however an Anglophile, and no friend to the pro-Communist left. This has led to his depiction by Kosta Vergopoulos as "the spokesman of the traditional oligarchy, which was openly hostile to the ambitions of the new bourgeoisie."[212] This is probably simplistic. Though outwardly sympathetic to its claims, he came profoundly to distrust the bloated and corrupt civil service. His later writings continued to be driven by an unvaried concern for the mass standard of living, and for the well-being of agriculture.[213] He mistrusted industrialisation. Recent Greek history had taught him that this was less a generator of popular well-being than a mechanism for diverting resources into a sector which merely raised the cost of living for ordinary people, through tariff protection and privileges.

British pressures[214] culminated in the foisting of Varvaressos upon a reluctant Voulgaris, who gave him the key supply portfolio as the basis for an attempt at monetary reform. Endowed with extraordinary powers, Varvaressos announced his reform programme on 5 June. Conceptually, his plan enjoyed intellectual coherence. It aimed at the partial expropriation of capitalistic wealth, and the building of a socially less unjust society. He presented his package as a recovery programme. Its aims transcended the mundane (but nonetheless more pressing) objective of stabilising fiscal and monetary imbalance. In practice, the broader aims proved irreconcilable with re-establishing monetary stability.

The main features of the Varvaressos reform included an attempt to suppress the free foreign exchange market, a scheme to reduce profits, the imposition of price maxima, and an extension of rationing. Olive oil was to be controlled by a state monopoly, to be applied not for fiscal reasons, but to cut its price at distribution. To assist the reform, Varvaressos secured the promise of an increase in UNRRA aid deliveries. This materialised but it provided no fiscal relief, since he slashed the price of relief supplies by 40 percent[215] from a level which already barely covered distribution costs. Both measures reflected his concern to cut the price of essentials, so as to minimise wage bargaining pressures.

Varvaressos also declared his intention to reduce the budget deficit by raising direct taxation. Subsequently he revealed his key fiscal measure. This was an "extraordinary contribution" on business, payable in nine monthly instalments. It was intended to raise 16 billion drachmas, within a budget intended to collect 78.2 billion and to spend 97 billion. The "contribution" was designed to mop up the redundant purchasing power of those who were already wealthy. These he equated with the business community *toute courte*, while regarding wages and salaries as being at subsistence level. The "contribution" was to be levied as a multiple of actual or imputed commercial and industrial rents. Makinen represents this tax as a device for clawing back the windfall to commercial tenants that resulted from rent control.[216] However, the tax was intended to be punitive as well as redistributive. At the time of its introduction, commercial rents in new drachmas were frozen at 1.5 times pre-war levels,[217] but in June, the price level stood at 12.17 times 1940. In its initial form, the tax rate differed between categories of business, ranging from 6 times rent, mainly for professional services, to 10 times and 15 times. The tax bands were widened at the end of July to a range of 3 times to 20 times.[218] This second schedule set taxes at 6 times rent for health professionals, through 15 times rent for cement works, tobacconists and taverns, to a top rate of 20 times rent for drapers, textile merchants and manufacturers, breweries, the olive oil trade and others.[219] On top of this, a clause in the legislation permitted local tax authorities to surcharge businesses over the prescribed tariff if they thought them capable of bearing a larger burden. This clause left assessment so wide open to abuse that Varvaressos later had to withdraw it. On the dubious assumption that rent control had enabled merchants to reap super-normal profits, they were not allowed to pass incidence of the tax on in prices. Market controls were imposed to force them to bear the entire incidence from their trading margins.

Let us assume that the equilibrium commercial rent had risen since 1940 parallel to prices generally, a very generous assumption considering that the volume of commerce was less than half of pre-war. On this basis, the highest rated group of businesses was being asked for a monthly tax payment of 20 x 12/9 x 1.5/12.17 times (i.e. 3.3 times) the market equilibrium rent on their premises, on top of the controlled rent they already paid. (According to Patterson, free market Athens area property values were about 20 times pre-war,[220] but this would not provide a valid proxy for equilibrium commercial rents, under high inflation).

There was a respectable case for introducing progressiveness into the tax system, and Varvaressos' "ingenious" contribution appears at first sight to have met this need. As merchants had to face a simultaneous cost squeeze, from a sharp statutory upward adjustment of employees wages, and a failure to control input prices, the impact of this tax on their earnings was potentially ferocious. Varvaressos' implied intention was indeed to impose a rate of more than 100 percent, since he later admitted that many enterprises would be unable to meet their tax liabilities out of the current net proceeds of sales. Rather, he hoped the tax would force merchants to sell "hoarded" commodities to meet tax liabilities."[221] Those who failed to comply were threatened with sequestration and imprisonment. UNRRA financial analyst Charles Coombes therefore regarded the "contribution" as a combination of capital levy and a tax on current incomes.[222]

Despite its inequities, there was, according to Gardner Patterson, "virtually no evidence of any significant liquidations of capital assets to meet the assessments."[223] However, the period during which the tax was implemented in its fullest rigour, with its incidence falling entirely on the merchant, lasted only till 1 September. On that date Varvaressos had to "recognise the difficulties of prompt payment," and give tax-payers till 10 September to pay their July and August levies.[224] By then, price control had been abandoned, and the real cost of the assessments fell sharply because of renewed inflation.

A second "extraordinary" - i.e. unrepeatable - tax, the Mantzavinos' war profits tax was retained, though its prospective yield was scaled down to 10 billion drachmas. It too was to fall on the business community. Into his budget Varvaressos also wrote a 10 billion drachma provision for the sale of "prizes of war," which was to yield exactly nothing. For all his insistence on hard money, Varvaressos' budget, which was unbalanced even at face value, was unlikely to establish fiscal stability. This could never be achieved without heavy indirect taxation and an attack on the bureaucracy. Varvaressos was unwilling to countenance the first, and half-hearted in confronting the civil servants.

Any mopping up of spending power that his penal tax regime on business might have achieved was massively offset by an across the board 50 percent rise in wage tariffs over May's level. Onto this was further grafted a provision for productivity bonuses. Civil Service salaries were raised on 1 June by 48 percent.[225] In real terms they were to continue rising in July, because of the 9.2 percent price deflation of that month. The aim was to restore wages, which, between March and May slipped by 39

81

percent in real terms. The cost-inflationary wage rise and the provision to slash the price of relief supplies seem eccentric, since only in January Varvaressos had spoken out both against excessive pay levels, and the under-pricing of relief deliveries. He was well aware of this, but he told Patterson that these sweeteners were necessary to consolidate labour support round his programme, which would fail without strong popular backing.[226] Moreover, the British Treasury endorsed this aspect of the plan.[227] Varvaressos had intended to offset part of the payroll cost by implementing the long deferred plan to sack occupation appointees from the civil service, of whom there were 15,846, or 20 percent of the payroll. He even had the redundancy notices issued, but he did not dare to implement them.[228]

The civil servants only accepted the wage rise grudgingly, but the aggressive populism of Varvaressos' measures won the "general approbation" he so eagerly sought. His strategy strongly reflected the advice of the British Treasury mandarins, who preached the gospel of controls to their Greek counterparts. Unlike Athens however, London disposed the necessary apparatus for intervention and the enforcement of its regulations.

The reform worked with spectacular success in the short run. Within a few days of Varvaressos' initial speech of 4 June, which signalled his determination to cut prices and raise taxation, the exchange rate of the drachma fell from 17,000 to the sovereign to 12,800. This anticipatory fall in the gold-exchange rate eased the passage of a sharp fall in prices. In part this was due to the 40 percent price cut on UNRRA rations, but non-ration prices also fell by 7 percent. At first sight this fall in non-ration prices is puzzling. A possible explanation is that Varvaressos promised future tough price controls, including administered price cuts, which were expected to be severe. Varvaressos told Leeper of his intention to reduce prices by 60 percent.[229] It is therefore possible that merchants tried to clear stock in anticipation of still lower administered prices, and to protect themselves from sanctions against hoarding, with which they were also threatened. In July, the deflationary environment was sustained by the new tax on commercial rents. It yielded 1.7 billion drachmas - not far short of the pro-rata monthly target of 1.77 billion, so it probably had its intended effect of forcing merchants to dump stock. This in tandem with the new salary rates caused a leap in real earnings. Between May and July, real government salaries soared by 57 percent, the real earnings index by 70 percent. The movements in post-liberation wages

fig. 6. (i)

Source: table A7.

are displayed above in figure 6.i. As this shows, wages moved wildly out of line with their longer term sustainable level. On the previous occasions when wages had risen so high, at the moment of liberation, and in March, the rates paid had also forced up the inflation rate - and they were to do the same again in December.

The reform generated the intense hostility of its prospective victims. Their grievances were sharpened by "serious injustices ... done by the government boards which assessed the taxes and set the maximum prices."[230] To enforce punitive price controls in the absence of disinflationary measures was far beyond the limited capacities of Varvaressos' staff. The black market flourished. By August, retailers' strikes began to spread. They were contained by threats of sanctions by the authorities, so increasing numbers of businessmen "altered tactics from that of outright refusal to sell to that of withholding under pretext of lack of stocks."[231] (Why "pretext"? If the tax worked in the way Varvaressos intended, stocks would be run down, and the June price fall indicates they probably were). In the olive oil trade, merchants connived with growers to withhold supplies. This created shortages and queuing. Black market prices surged.[232] In August, receipts from the extraordinary tax on business fell to 1.3 billion drachmas. The UNRRA representative foresaw a further shrinkage of yields, doubting whether the tax would raise more in all than 5-10 billion drachmas. This would lead to an unanticipated revenue shortfall of 6 - 10 billion drachmas. The yield of the retrospective tax on war profits would fall a further 7 - 8 billion behind target. Given that the 10 billion of revenue expected from "prizes of war" was pure window dressing, the budget deficit still had to be covered by heavy new emissions of paper.

The Varvaressos reform has attracted retrospective admiration especially on the part of Greek writers. They argue (as did Varvaressos himself) that it failed because the state apparatus was unable to enforce his price controls and the new property tax. In most texts on the Greek hyperinflation, space is devoted to holding up unpatriotic bourgeois greed as the scapegoat for fiscal failure. Moralising, is however, no substitute for analysis. Success was to depend on the compliance of better-off tax-payers with measures designed specifically to ruin them. This was guaranteed to provoke resistance. In fact the tax was so riddled with inequities and disincentives that British advisers got the Greek government to change it fundamentally in the Spring of 1946.[233]

The Varvaressos tax regime created a massive surge in the real value of revenue between May and August from 239 million (1940) drachmas to 485 million. Yet it failed badly in its aim of balancing the budget, because expenditure advanced (again in real terms) from 462 million to 844 million. Monthly government revenue and expenditure of governments following the liberation is displayed as table 6.1. (see p. 86).

The May-Aug. 1945 surge in expenditure seems largely to have been caused by the hoisting of civil service pay. The price paid to organised labour may have been necessary to secure popular support, but it was high enough to wreck the stability the reform was supposed to bring, even if the tax and price control regimes could have been made to stick.

Not surprisingly, inflation soon resumed. On September 1, Varvaressos resigned "discouraged by failure,"[234] attacking the "economic oligarchy." In fact he was almost certainly pushed, for Patterson notes that on stepping down he became so isolated politically that he deemed it wise to leave the country. A berth was eventually found for him at the World Bank.[235] He nevertheless calculated that the chaos which would ensue would force his re-instatement.[236] The gains he contrived for labour were quickly obliterated, as the new wage tariff was overwhelmed by renewed inflation from late August onward. The real wage index crashed back in September by 31-32 percent. This did not stabilise the price level, however.

TABLE 6.1.

	GOVERNMENT REVENUE AND SPENDING AFTER THE LIBERATION					
	Government		Consumer prices	Real		
	Spending	Revenue		expenditure	Revenue	deficit
	m. drachmas					
Nov-44	1232	71	1.51	815	47	768
Dec-44	611	15	10.94	56	1	54
Jan-45	1832	41	8.62	212	5	208
Feb-45	2743	177	7.27	377	24	353
Mar-45	5150	1572	6.29	819	250	569
Apr-45	4906	1784	8.38	585	213	373
May-45	5417	2801	11.72	462	239	223
Jun-45	6901	3259	12.17	567	268	299
Jul-45	8062	6050	11.05	729	547	182
Aug-45	9448	5429	11.19	844	485	359
Sep-45	11080	5973	16.26	681	367	314
Oct-45	14082	7167	25.70	548	279	269
Nov-45	18941	10511	41.02	462	256	206
Dec-45	40441	15254	77.55	522	197	325
Jan-46	50449	22487	165.8	304	136	169
Feb-46	114467	41802	142.3	804	294	510
Mar-46	192986	65864	145.4	1327	453	874
Apr-46	150954	69981	148.5	1016	471	545
May-46	214764	94822	150.4	1428	631	798
Jun-46	76774	91842	150.7	509	609	-100
Jul-46	142615	129035	149.7	953	862	91
Aug-46	139175	117843	145.1	959	812	147
Sep-46	133456	153780	149.9	891	1026	-136
Oct-46	140901	169449	154.5	912	1097	-185
Nov-46	182687	155252	160.3	1140	968	171
Dec-46	269336	169167	151.1	1783	1120	663

Sources: to 10/11/44, Patterson, Thesis, p. 27.
11/11/44-Dec 46: Bank of Greece, *Monthly statistical reports* Nov. 46-Jan 48, table 20.
1/45 spending (1832m dr.) Patterson, Thesis, p. 102. Receipts: 41 million.
12/44-1/45 expenditure 2443 receipts 56. Bank of Greece.

Chapter 7. The fourth "End": The Anglo Greek Financial Agreement and its aftermath

Admiral Voulgaris was a conviction free marketer. His stance caused amusement at the British Treasury, which regarded economic liberalism as an ante-diluvian doctrine. He was not sorry to see Varvaressos go, and replaced him as supply minister with Ioannis Paraskevopoulos. The new minister agreed in principle with Varvaressos' price control policy, but deemed it unworkable till the state had brought commodity supply under its own control. Accordingly, while promising no change in policy, the administration "temporarily" lifted price controls on 6 September to re-supply the market.[237] At a stroke therefore Paraskevopoulos converted the "contribution" into an indirect tax, eliminating its essential progressiveness. Over time other adjustments nibbled away at the Varvaressos tax, though it continued to provide a modest flow of revenue. A renewed burst of inflation was inevitable. The fiscal balance rapidly deteriorated, as the Tanzi effect, that is to say, the in-built tendency of inflation to reduce the ex-post purchasing power of tax receipts, once more began biting deeply into revenue.[238] As the authorities feared to raise the price of relief goods, the deficits could only be covered by new currency creation.

Most Greek politicians clung as an article of faith to the belief that prosperity would be restored by the generosity of outside donors and debtors, rather than by domestic efforts. An air of fatalistic fantasy overhung financial discussion. For example, Varvaressos had repeatedly and without foundation announced the imminent arrival of a $240 million bonanza he expected from the Americans. Later, when asked in October to file their reparations claim against Germany, the Greeks came up with a fanciful demand for $10.5 billion, or 19.6 times their 1939 domestic product.[239] They subsequently raised this demand to $15.8 billion - at 1938 prices - but eventually had to settle for $2.7 million of grossly overvalued German assets in kind.[240]

Britain became increasingly impatient with the Greek political leadership. The Treasury "doubted whether any country in the world has, at the moment, such a generally favourable basis for reconstruction and recovery." It carried no internal debt. It was not servicing its foreign obligations. It was receiving imports by volume at 50 percent above the pre-war rate. It held £40 million in reserves, and its security was underwritten by Britain, which was making heavy sacrifices for Greece's benefit.[241]

At the beginning of November 1945, the government coalition split apart and Voulgaris tendered his resignation. The Regent, Archbishop Damaskinos, installed a new government under Panayotis Kanellopoulos. The new finance minister, Gregorios Kasimatis, submitted his own programme for stabilisation. Kasimatis was an economic liberal and had been a vehement opponent of Varvaressos. He wanted to scrap Varvaressos' panoply of controls, and to induce recovery through encouragement of the private sector.[242] As usual, the programme depended on a plea for foreign assistance. The centre-piece of Kasimatis' programme was a plan to dump a million gold sovereigns on the market to stabilise the drachma exchange rate. Of these, 650,000 would have to be imported from Britain. Kasimatis was effectively trying to repeat the seigniorage maximisation technique which had been applied by Neubacher in 1943-44. Pro-forma compliance with budget balancing was written into the programme. Luxury taxes and the prices of relief supplies were to be raised, but Kasimatis "regarded his gold project as the key to success."[243] Whitehall flatly rejected this plan, both in original and in a re-drafted form, which reluctantly shifted emphasis towards budget balancing, but without abandoning the gold project. After talks with the Americans, who persuaded him to drop the gold sales and concentrate on the budget, Kasimatis announced his package of tax increases and the re-pricing of relief goods. Prices were to be stabilised by controls, and by (the hope of) greater UNRRA deliveries. Constrained by pressure from Whitehall not to devalue the drachma from its now grotesque formal parity, he also promised to make more hard currency available to importers at the official rate.

The resources with which to implement the Kasimatis plan were wholly lacking. No British loan was in prospect. To Kasimatis' plea for assistance, the British government replied that Britain had "already scraped the bottom of the barrel to provide aid for Greece.[244] Ominously, donor fatigue also threatened a drying up of the UNRRA relief on which the Greek economic system, such as it was, depended. All the British could offer was a team of advisers to breathe down the necks of the Greek spending agencies, together with proposals for a state lottery and a blitz on the black market. They also wanted the Greeks to start nationalising industry.[245]

On Nov. 19, the Kanellopoulos government was replaced with a left of centre coalition headed by Themistocles Sophoulis. This was a result of intense pressure exerted by British ambassador Rex Leeper on Regent

Damaskinos. Leeper's concern was to try at all costs to exclude the Royalists from power.[246] The Sophoulis government's remit was to accept the British economic advisers and tackle the budget deficit. That at least was what the British understood. However, despite now rampant hyperinflation (59.6 percent in November, and rising fast) the Greeks still declined to balance the budget until a new tranche of foreign aid was in the bag. A tax rise, they claimed, would over-strain the Greek economy. Another stabilisation was now unavoidable, because of the intensity of the flight from the drachma into gold, and because of the operation of the Tanzi effect on the revenue. Though decreeing (at Leeper's behest) the restriction of gold dealings,[247] vice-premier Emmanuel Tsouderos began from 1 December to put into effect Kasimatis' plan to sell sovereigns from the reserves of the Bank of Greece.[248] The release of gold was too small significantly to restrain the soaring rate of exchange, which out-paced the vertiginous ascent of the price level.[249] In all 150,000 sovereigns were released for this purpose by liberation governments in 1944 and 1945. They were equivalent to about 3 percent of the estimated stock of gold in private hands. This sounds a mere drop in the bucket, but during those months when government gold was sold, its volume was comparable to that which had been sold by the Germans earlier.[250]

As a diplomatic tactic, letting inflation rip succeeded. On 21 December, supply minister Georgios Kartalis warned Leeper that without more foreign assistance, the Greek economy would descend into chaos.[251] The familiar symptoms of hyperinflationary collapse began to show: local produce vanished from the market, because of "the general unwillingness to sell for drachmas in which nobody had any confidence."[252] Very reluctantly, London, pressed both by the Greeks for aid, and by the Americans for a positive response to their calls, consented to bring Tsouderos and Kartalis to London to discuss a development aid and stabilisation package. The Greeks entered the talks emphasising that "reconstruction must have priority over stabilisation," to the irritation of the British who resented Greek "dictation" for a "scheme which will get them out of all their troubles."[253]

Even when the Greek ministers arrived in London on 1 January 1946, the British authorities had still not agreed as to how to deal with their demands. A week later, Tsouderos was "being fobbed off with discussions on programmes and plans,"[254] while the mandarins of Treasury, Foreign Office and Bank of England debated what to do. The deadlock had eventually to be broken on 22 January by Foreign Secretary Ernest Bevin who issued a 24 hour deadline for completion of negotiations.[255]

The Foreign Office had formulated its own stabilisation plan for Greece, which the Treasury and the Bank of England regarded as economically illiterate. Foreign office minister Hector McNeil's financial adviser, Mr. Grove, formerly of Lazards Bank, argued that gold was for Greece already the "real" means of exchange. It should therefore be given that status *de jure*.[256] It was useless for the Greeks to try to balance their budget unless the currency were already stable. So they should convert their entire currency supply into gold. This would still leave them with £1.7 million (gold) as a "cushion," on which they could draw while putting the new budget measures into force.[257]

Grove's plan was "accepted in principle," by the Foreign Office, though the Bank of England was implacably opposed to it. Foreign Office backing was probably assured by the energetic support it received from Ambassador Leeper. By putting Greece on a sovereign standard, pure and simple, control of the money supply would be removed from the reach of the Greek government. However, the latter (whom Leeper regarded as his protégé) had to be "assured of allied support in the future,"[258] for it was "of great importance that the present government should be maintained in power until the March elections,"[259] presumably to give it a better chance of winning them.

The Treasury was less enthusiastic, but both its brain-children, the Waley and Varvaressos stabilizations, had collapsed so "no effective alternative appeared to be available."[260] In discussions with the Foreign Office, the Treasury, represented by Sir Wilfrid Eady, offered no coherent strategy, but was attracted to any plan which could "prevent a complete collapse" of the drachma in the short term. Then, during the six week run-up to the Greek elections, the Bank of Greece could continue to sell sovereigns[261] - i.e. Leeper's protégés were to be kept in power, and if possible, helped by the stabilisation to win the election. On the other hand, "proposals for introducing a gold metallic currency for Greece based on the sovereign should be abandoned." Indeed, the Treasury deemed it more desirable to engineer a rise in the drachma against gold, to make the drachma worth holding. Moreover, the Greek government should not be given "the slightest idea that it is possible" that Britain would "maintain the Greek economy indefinitely at our own expense," because "they will then refrain from taking the necessary but unpopular measures to put their own house in order."[262]

Waley, who was "put in charge of Greece" at the Treasury,[263] was implacably opposed, not only to the Grove plan, but to any form of drachma convertibility. Having spent his war advising on exchange control arrangements, he warned against permitting the renewed international movement of hot-money, which "everybody had come to feel ... was extremely anti-social." Therefore "capital flights should not be allowed in the future." If "rich Greeks" converted their drachmas to harder currency, the Greek government would lose its reserves, and a new crisis would arrive.[264] So he returned to his theme of a year previously: the Greeks needed to do much more for themselves. The UNRRA deliveries could not be increased, for Greece was already getting more than her fair share. The budget had to be balanced, and wages strictly controlled. Although taxation methods should favour social justice, it was counterproductive to remove the incentive for industrialists to produce.[265] Waley entertained no strong objection to the use of gold as an aid to stabilisation on the basis of a truly balanced budget (which he thought "unlikely in the present circumstances") but to set up a gold backed currency was "the most wasteful way of using gold."[266]

The Bank of England also recognised "the dangers of offering convertibility to any note holder," but warned Waley that if convertibility were made subject to Greek exchange control, this "might cause a breakdown of the new arrangements at the outset". Knowing this had to be a sore point with Waley, it questioned whether HM Government (i.e. the Treasury) "could afford a third failure?" Waley remained unconvinced.[267] However, the Governor of the Bank saw no prospect of the new Greek currency maintaining its stability without full convertibility.[268]

Relations between Foreign Office and Treasury became highly charged, with the Bank trying to hold the ring. Eventually the Foreign Office dropped the Grove plan. This was as much because of the tactlessness of its author as for its intrinsic absurdity. Grove thereupon predicted that any alternative arrangement would be unacceptable to the Greek government, and that the country would lapse into chaos. This would necessitate large scale British military intervention. (In fact Tsouderos would have rejected the Grove plan himself, since it would "impugn the credit and prestige of the Bank of Greece,"[269] such as they were). Waley on the other hand had to concede limited convertibility for the drachma, though the Treasury remained adamantly opposed to giving Greece guarantees on its exchange rate which might involve a drain on sterling.[270] The outcome was an arrangement in which the Bank of Greece would convert drachmas to foreign exchange "for imports and other approved purposes."

There was however, agreement that Greece should get a small British loan. No such loan was really needed, since Greece still had a plentiful reserve of sterling, but the loan was structured in such a way as to provide (nominal) cover for the drachma. Its purpose was solely to allow the Greek negotiators on their return to show they had secured something tangible for their country, and "as a lever to force them to behave sensibly over their own finances".[271]

From these tortured internal negotiations, certain points of consensus emerged, which formed the body of the agreement. Firstly, despite Treasury misgivings, gold support must be available for the drachma, to shore up the incumbent administration. However, no formal undertaking could be given as to its convertibility. Secondly, the Greeks must not be allowed to expect further British assistance if the stabilisation foundered. In the upshot, two loans were granted to Greece, the first of £10 million from the UK, and the second of $25 million from the US Export-Import Bank. This was far less than the Greeks had hoped for, but London estimated that it was "more than sufficient" to stabilise the currency.[272] It was also unnecessary. The Greek government had not been able to spend its sterling credits, which had swollen from the £37 million remaining after the fall of Greece to more than £50 million, on account of credits in respect of £BMA and drachmas expended in Greece by the British army. As a further sweetener in the Anglo-Greek agreement, the British government waived its claim to return of the £46 million debt incurred by Greece in 1940-41 (without a counterpart renunciation by the Greeks of the sterling credits) so just as in 1918, Greece re-emerged from World War 2 as a substantial creditor to Britain. Keynes, at the Treasury, grappling with the apparently intractable problem of the sterling balances, told Waley that it was "perfectly preposterous" for Britain to "give still further gratuitous relief to a country to whom at present we owe more than £50 million." Rather, the unavoidable assistance on which Greece would continue to draw for food supplies and her military needs - which he estimated for 1946 at £24 million - should be debited against her till her sterling balances were exhausted.[273]

Under the Anglo-Greek Financial Agreement, the Greeks devalued the drachma and undertook "gradually" to reduce the budget deficits."[274] However the agreement did not lead to the fiscal stringency normally associated with a "final" stabilisation. Hugh Dalton, British Chancellor of the Exchequer, feared with justification that in the hands of "Tsouderos and Co.," Britain's £10 million would be "thrown down the drain."[275] He was not far wrong. Between February and May 1946, Greek government policy entered an Epicurean phase.

This profligacy received tacit British Foreign Office encouragement. For the British it was more desirable to manipulate un-elected Greek politicians than to deal with an elected Royalist regime, but on the other it could hardly endorse the protracted denial of representative government for Greece, while calling for democracy in Soviet controlled Europe. So, because of British pressure, Premier Sophoulis could not escape fixing the date for Greece's first post-war election. This was to be held at the end of March. He expected to lose to the Royalists, and therefore tried to postpone it, but the British would not let him flout the rules so blatantly.[276] Still, he wanted to maximise his chances. So spending doubled from the 1945 monthly (real) average of 567 million 1940 drachmas to 1144 million a month, and the real deficit soared from 307 million to 682 million.

In themselves therefore, the promise of aid and the problematic expectation of tougher financial discipline could not have terminated Greece's last bout of extreme inflation. The decisive factor was that the market believed correctly that the British would let the Bank of Greece support the drachma exchange rate by selling sovereigns it bought in London with Greece's reserve gold. Tsouderos returned to Athens with 500,000 sovereigns in his baggage, and the "full but reluctant" assent of the UK Treasury to their sale to support the drachma.[277] Gold sales began in secrecy in January 1946 and openly from February onward, to hold the drachma at about 130,000 to the sovereign. It was held at around this rate for the rest of the year. The intensity of gold sales needed to support the drachma surpassed all precedent. In May another 500,000 sovereigns were secured from the USA, and as many again were promised by London. This permitted 1946 gold sales to swallow 2.1 million sovereigns, double the quantity sold by the Germans in 1944.[278]

This rate of disposal was unsustainable. The gold reserve, as taken out in 1941, was equivalent to 608,350 oz. at standard fineness, and capable of being minted to 2,369,000 sovereigns.[279] Of these 450,000 had been brought to Greece shortly after the liberation, and had mostly been sold at the end of 1944. Sales in November 1945 - January 1946 had run to 97,000 sovereigns. So gold sales in 1946 effectively wiped out the Greek metallic reserve, and could only be sustained by intermittent borrowing from the USA. The increased rate of new money emission, which was made possible by the maintenance of the exchange rate and domestic prices, was also unsustainable in the absence of official gold sales. Real money supply rose sharply, though to a less spectacular extent than the deficit, but that was only because part of that deficit was financed by selling sovereigns.

This carefree spending boom sustained prosperity during the run-up to the free election at the end of March 1946. Despite it, the Populists (i.e. Royalists) led by Konstantinos Tsaldaris won the election, as expected. However, the spending boom continued till May because it took time for the British economic advisers and the new currency committee to establish themselves. Only in mid April did serious budget planning begin.[280] According to W H McNeill, the advisers, from the start of their mission, found their endeavours to be frustrated by passive resistance by the Greek administration, and the cavalier attitude to fiscal rectitude became even more blatant under the Tsaldaris government. The budget it presented in June that year was only balanced on the basis of heroic assumptions on the revenue side, so as to induce British and US officials to approve further loan requests.[281] There is an element of exaggeration and left-wing bias in McNeill's account, for the statistical evidence (table 6.1, above) contradicts this statement. British fiscal influence did gradually predominate and deficits dropped sharply from June onwards. That month probably marks the true ending of the hyperinflationary regime.

The price level remained steady till the end of 1946, but this did not inaugurate a period of stability. Gold sales had to continue. To the British, selling gold was a regrettable expedient whose sole aim was to buy time for fiscal reform to progress. To the Greeks, it performed the same function as Neubacher's Gold Action in 1944. It enhanced the drachma as a source of seigniorage, since stability led to a strong recovery in hand to hand cash balances. It therefore permitted fiscal improvement to be offset by a rapid expansion in bank lending, particularly for agriculture.[282] As bank deposits remained insignificant, most of the credit was created by the Bank of Greece. It rapidly augmented the money supply. Moreover, the authorities pursued a policy of import maximisation and export suppression, to counter domestic dissatisfaction. This dissipated the reserves of foreign currency. Gardner Patterson, who served on the Currency Committee, argued that little had changed fundamentally; in the absence of sustained gold sales, inflation would have taken off again. Indeed, according to his account, Greece was in a desperate condition by the end of 1946. Its reserves were on the point of exhaustion, just at the time when the Communist insurgency in the north was gaining serious momentum.

From this aspect, the announcement of the Truman Doctrine, and on 12 March 1947 the explicit inclusion of Greece in the front line of America's response to Communist expansion was felicitously timed. It promised a massive inflow of resources. The worst of the civil war still lay in the future, and the defence of a still inflationary drachma was to require further sales of about 2 million sovereigns between 1947 and 1950,[283] despite which the cost of living rose 97.3 percent between 1946 and 1951. There is little evidence throughout this period that the January 1946 reform changed the "rules of the game" more fundamentally than had the earlier stabilisation attempts of Waley and Varvaressos.

Chapter 8. The four "ends:" An interpretation

Most authors who deal with Greece in 1941-46 focus either on the occupation or on the post liberation period and perceive a clean break between them. This study however emphasises continuity in financial policy across the period as a whole. Neither the German authorities in Greece nor their later British counterparts could induce client Greek governments to stabilise their finances. During the occupation, the Greeks resisted the imposition of taxation supposedly because it might be used as payment to the occupation authorities. They continued to resist it after the liberation. In both periods, Greek governments tried to use the tax system mainly to extract revenue from the business community, on a hit or miss basis which usually missed. They avoided taxation whose incidence might fall on the urban consumer. So they raised very little revenue.

The Axis administration soon realised it would be a waste of effort to get the Greek government to balance its accounts. It therefore orientated its currency policy towards the maximisation of seigniorage. This was necessary both for the extraction of the occupation levy, and for the functioning of the Greek government. Neubacher's first initiative, the reform of November 1942, exploited (highly successfully) the turn round in public expectations on the future value of the drachma. It yielded an enhanced flow of seigniorage at more or less stable prices for five or six months. In the absence of a fiscal stabilisation, very high inflation resumed in the late summer of 1943. By October, the consequent contraction in hand to hand balances threatened to destroy the base for inflation tax. So, in November 1943, policy switched to selling gold. This maintained enough confidence in the drachma for the printing press to yield a continued flow of seigniorage. By the late summer of 1944 the demand for hand to hand money shrank too much for seigniorage to provide adequate non-fiscal revenue. So the Germans considered the "Rentendrachma" plan, which would again furnish the authorities with seigniorage. Neubacher thought it bound to fail, but had no suggestions of his own to offer when refused a further supply of gold.

The in-coming Greek liberation authorities must have been impressed with the apparent ease with which the Axis occupiers had extracted taxless revenue. No explicit reference is made in the literature to what, if anything, they learned from the financial management of the occupation period. Patterson, when I interviewed him, denied that he had ever heard

Greek officials refer to Axis economic policy, except in wholly negative terms. True, Neubacher and Hahn had conducted their operations secretively, without involving Greek officials, except finance minister Hector Tsironikas, whose discretion they trusted.[284] Still, the market was aware of what they were doing. So too were the British authorities, from the reports that reached them from Greece. Unfortunately, they wrongly discounted this information as being "not too reliable,"[285] but Waley was given a reasonably accurate resumé of German financial policy during the occupation from Greek officials at an informal lunch.[286] The immediacy with which the newly landed Greek finance ministry and Bank of Greece officials demanded gold from London, not to buy goods directly, but to support the drachma, suggests that the Greeks still hankered after the previous scheme of financial management, under the more favourable conditions created by the British military presence. Like their discredited predecessors, who were consigned to Greek gaols from which they did not emerge alive, the new managers needed this means of preserving their seigniorage.

As the liberation governments preferred not to tax if they could avoid it, the months that followed the stabilisation of November 1944 witnessed a replay of Neubacher's November 1942 stabilisation. By April 1945, the accumulation of transactions balances could no longer absorb new emissions. This led to Varvaressos' reform in June. Its principal feature was a punitive raid on business, to force the release of inventories (the lynchpin of the earlier Neubacher reform) while buying popular support with cheap food and wage increases. The consequent boost to real incomes was so great as to destabilise the package. Varvaressos tried to contain the disequilibrium with administrative controls but his civil servants proved incapable of implementing them. On the collapse of his reform, his successors reverted to the Neubacher technique of 1944 - seigniorage maximisation with the assistance of gold sales. The illusion of distress created by renewed inflation secured Greece new finance from Britain and the USA. Rather than re-balance spending with revenue, the Greeks dug deep into their gold and hard currency reserves both to procure a further rich harvest of seigniorage, and to secure popular well-being through the growth of imports.

Post-liberation governments are depicted in the literature as compelled by weakness and insecurity to avoid mass taxation. Their prime concern was to pacify the urban masses, because their survival was threatened by the militancy of organised labour. This interpretation needs revision. Before the Battle of Athens (December 1944) finance was controlled by E.A.M socialist group ministers. Their policies were tailored specifically to the interest of organised labour. After the E.A.M.-ELAS putsch was crushed however, the armed left was seriously weakened and for most of 1945 there was no urgent need to appease it. However, it remained British policy, and that of ambassador Rex Leeper in particular, to bolster what Leeper called a "Left-Centre" in Greece. This was to block the ambitions of the Right - Royalist or Republican - to crush the Communists, for fear that this might renew the civil war. As he puts it, "British influence was always exerted towards broadening the government, which in fact meant incorporating within it representatives of parties further to the left."[287] Leeper's immense discretionary powers were commented on after the fall of Plastiras in April 1945 by his United States counterpart McVeagh. "I told Leeper the other day that he ought to make a collection of "Prime Ministers I have tried."[288] Leaving open the question whether it was "British" influence or Leeper's own vice-regal policy making at work, this also meant bringing down administrations and replacing them whenever it seemed the Right might assert control of them. These administrations therefore competed with the Communists for the loyalties of employees, including their own civil service, in order to build a power base strong enough to ward off pressures from the Right. However, as Leeper reluctantly admitted, the experience of the Battle of Athens so far polarised Greek politics that Left-Centrism attracted little support. The administrations fashioned in the light of this concept were excessively anxious to promote the cause of labour, to woo this constituency away from the Communists. Consequently, on the spending side, they tried to minimise food prices, and to reward their bureaucracy and fledgling army on relatively generous terms.

It was not fear of labour which drove them in this direction. If they had chosen to adopt a tougher line with organised labour, they could probably have succeeded. The cost of such a policy would have been to seek right wing support. This was anathema to them, or at least to Leeper. The rank and file support for Communist militancy was less than solid. In June 1945, while Varvaressos was implementing his programme to buy off labour as the condition for monetary reform, the left-wing Salonica local authority was faced with the threat of a general strike. So it insouciantly conceded utility workers a pay rise of 125 percent. The utility enterprise lacked the funds to meet the settlement. Thereupon the utility workers struck. The company responded with a promise of 50 percent. As it had as yet no funds to finance this offer, the union turned it down. But "it was clear that these workers lacked militancy beyond a certain point, as military and substitute labour were introduced apparently without incidents."[289]

A more serious confrontation with organised labour developed after the resignation of Varvaressos. The Voulgaris government, which was beginning to move in a right-ward direction, had to face a mounting strike wave, initiated by textile workers in Piraeus. It was surprised by this because it supposed (illogically) that its measures to re-supply commodity markets (by ending price fixing) would "take the edge off the strikers' case." Notionally, the strike was for better wages and shorter hours. However, the (British) economic adviser's office demonstrated that this was the second in a run of strikes which were timed to prevent the re-opening of textile capacity. It concluded "ineluctably" that "the Communist party, under the existing political regime, prefers the workers to be out of work."[290] It may be doubted whether the rank and file much cared to be deployed for this purely strategic objective. The authorities refused in the face of the gathering Communist led strike-wave to compensate labour for the real wage shrinkage caused by the decontrol of consumer prices. The strikes collapsed.[291]

It was not organised labour that brought the government down shortly afterwards. Rather Voulgaris was unwilling to lose his left-wing ministers and to depend largely on the Right. This was coupled with intense pressure by Leeper to rebuild a left leaning administration.[292] Similarly, the frequent initiatives to sack civil servants all foundered as long as implementation remained in the hands of the liberation era governments. However, when the Populist (Royalist) Tsaldaris government won power through the ballot, it made its own civil service purge - now directed against the Left - effective.[293] It was not government weakness vis-à-vis powerful organised labour which prevented the liberation governments from balancing their budgets, rather their desperate search for an anti-Royalist consensus which barely existed.

Taxation was applied only in the hope of extracting wealth from the business community. It was easy to create a left leaning consensus around the proposition that businessmen were the only people in Greece who commanded resources above those necessary for biological survival. Moreover, the public could easily be persuaded that business was a parasitic activity.[294] So business earnings, real, imputed, or imaginary, were fair game for the tax collector. Even firms uncontaminated by active collaboration were held to have profited from the occupation, and so to have acquired funds which the state claimed the moral title to tax retrospectively.[295] The Liberals, nominally representing the business interest in the various centre-left leaning coalitions, knew that their own supporters would have to carry the entire burden of taxation. They were therefore the most enthusiastic in urging the need for a foreign loan with which to carry the expense of government during the transitional period. No such assistance was forthcoming. As Greek governments, despite the horde of under-employed civil servants on the pay-roll, lacked equitable and efficient mechanisms for taxing and regulating business, and as business was capable of defending its own interests, very little tax revenue could be raised.

Therefore post-restoration governments tried to survive on seigniorage, always pleading the indigence of all but the (unpatriotic) businessmen. The collaborationist politicians had differed from the legitimate in their foreign policy stance, but all were drawn from the same social-political stratum. Lacking the independence of landed wealth, they had colonised the state and the institutions. Independent business wealth threatened their perquisites and prestige. So too, did the expansion of a Communist backed labour movement. By trying to hit at business, governments could pander to popular opinion. A Marxist explanation is that by stifling capitalistic growth, they would impede the expansion of its antithesis, the rise of the proletariat.[296]

Since governments needed both to protect the salariat, and to win the assent of organised labour, they were usually concerned to raise real wages, or to alter the distribution of income in labour's favour. Especially in late 1944 and again in the summer of 1945, wage raising policies de-stabilised efforts otherwise directed to the control of inflation. The government spending bill was made up overwhelmingly of wage payments. As civil service labour was perennially dissatisfied with its conditions of employment (including its pensions) and as it strenuously resisted redundancies, the need to pacify it destabilised budgets and stimulated excess demand.

During the earlier years of Axis control, government efforts had been limited to protecting the well-being of state officials, but after the real income collapse of late 1943 and early 1944, the partisan threat led them to seek broader support by conceding the allocation of wages in kind. Later, in the face of imminent political collapse, they bade for popularity by augmenting the wage in kind, by letting money wages rip, and by packing the official payrolls. This caused an extraordinary rise in real wages, which aggravated already extreme inflation. The liberation governments tried to sustain these high wage levels, directly by setting high official wage tariffs, and indirectly by misusing food aid. Renewed inflation diluted the effects of wage raising, but the policy reached its apotheosis in Varvaressos' reform. This again caused real wages to leap to unsustainable levels, wrecking his effort to re-balance the budget.

When real wages were driven up by government action (in late 1942, in the autumn and winter of 1944, and in June 1945) this was always achieved by forcing the depletion of inventories. This process was inherently transient. The interludes of price stability and high wages were unsustainable. Deficit financing, combined with the exhaustion of inventories, kept cutting real wages back to more sustainable levels. The compensatory wage increases which attended the renewal of hyperinflation were insufficient to maintain real wage levels, and to this extent wage trends should have damped the inflation cycle. However, renewed inflation itself weakened fiscal discipline, through the loss in value of revenue receipts during the collection period. No appropriate monetary measures were applied to offset fiscal laxity.

Ultimately, the Greek hyperinflation persisted over its extraordinarily long 56 month course because successive governments kept finding new means of reviving the flow of seigniorage. Figure 8 (i) on p. 102 plots both the volume of real money balances in the economy and the volume of seigniorage extracted, month by month over the entire inflation and immediate post-stabilisation period. Not for a single month did the authorities stop extracting seigniorage in very large volume, (except in December 1944, when they could not get access to the banknote stocks). The periods which followed all the cosmetic stabilizations (including that of January 1946) were those in which the printing presses were driven most vigorously, in terms of the real spending power procured thereby. Indeed, the currency was used throughout - with considerable skill - as a machine for seigniorage maximisation.

Figure 8(i)

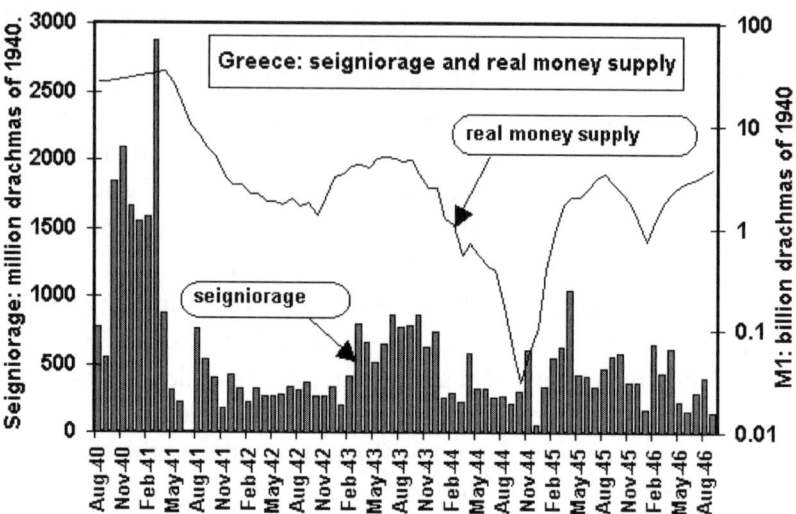

Source: Table A5.

The interventions made over this period (four cosmetic stabilizations and three programmes of gold-sales) sufficed periodically to restore enough short-run public confidence in the drachma to maintain the seigniorage maximisation policy. Without these interventions, the pace of inflation would have reached such heights as to have led to public refusal to accept newly printed currency notes in return for goods and services rendered. Just such a crisis briefly threatened in early November 1944, and recurred in December 1945, each time lending urgency to search for a stabilisation formula.

The Greek officials who administered the economy did not understand what they were doing in terms of their dependence on seigniorage. Nobody, for example, ever admitted "we have no interest in achieving conventional monetary equilibrium, because it is politically more expedient to finance the state and economic recovery by printing the money, than to cut spending, restrain wages, and reform the taxation system." It is unlikely that they ever thought that this was what they were doing. Unfortunately, it was not always clear what they really did think. When Greek sources introduced a "theoretical" component into their discussion of macro-economic or financial matters, they sometimes lapsed into an impenetrable jargon. The British were never quite certain how best to deal with their Greek counterparts - "theorists only and not men of action."[297] To some extent "theory" was used by them as an exercise in evasion, as the British indeed supposed. However, what passed among educated Greeks for "theory" could descend at worst into undisciplined intellectualism, detached from the empiricism which has to inform the practice of positive economics. The British were also exasperated at the casual way in which Greek officials carried out their duties. The casually compiled post-liberation budgets and budget revisions were only drawn up disdainfully as window dressing in response to pressures from foreign officials to ensure a continued or enhanced flow of assistance.

It is hard to find evidence that the administrators discerned any link between governmental deficits and their inflationary consequences. They avoided this issue by proceeding from a different standpoint. To run the country meant to incur politically or morally inescapable expenditures. The mass of the people were too poor to pay for government, so there was no point in asking them to do so. Anybody who had money must have made it by collaborating and by "speculation," but this class was too wily to be taxed. So it was up to the foreigner to pay up, for he "owed" the Greeks a decent living to recompense their heroism and sacrifices during the war. If prices rose, this indicated a shortfall between the legitimate expectations of the Greek people and the inadequate inflow of assistance from abroad.

An incident which illustrates the inclination of the Greeks to blame the British for their difficulties arose out of a reason given by Varvaressos in May 1945 for not devaluing the drachma. He was "very distressed at the thought that British troops might receive more drachmae if the rate was altered."[298] Except perhaps for ELAS supporters, the Greeks did not regard the British army as an occupation force like the Axis garrisons. It was nonetheless the object of increasing jealousy, to which the army was sensitive. Concern for Greek welfare had led already to intense propaganda by the army to encourage saving by the troops. They were enjoined not to compete for commodities which were needed by the Greeks themselves, even though off-base troop spending was largely confined to wine, women and song, none of which were in short supply. Varvaressos' complaint was acted on, but the forces representative reported in August that propaganda was delivering decreasing results among the troops. "In rich areas of Athens and in many country districts, they see the Greeks feeding quite well, and well dressed.... In many respects they find out on home leave that their families are far worse off than the Greeks." The feeling in the military became widespread that "the Greeks are being given far too much relief, in the way of foodstuffs at any rate."[299]

Since the combination of persiflage, dilettantism and insistent demands for help exasperated the British officials with whom the Greeks had to liaise, then conversely, Varvaressos' unusual clarity of thought was an important reason for the insufficiently critical foreign admiration he enjoyed. He was energetic. He seemed to understand Greece's problems. His plan of June 1945 seemed internally consistent with the ends he had set himself. The fact that his "ingenious" programme was intrinsically unworkable would only become apparent with hindsight. Its failure would be attributed not to its intrinsic defects, but to "speculators," or to the machinations of the "selfish and superficial ... economic oligarchy," or (variously) to the "mob in the streets," and the lack of competent staff to police his measures.

Greece and the Gold Bug

The role of the gold sovereign was clearly critical to the financial management of Greece during the inflation period. The stock of gold in private hands was hugely increased during the period 1941-46, as Table 8.1. below (expressed in million £ gold) shows, and was set to rise still further to 12.55m by 1951.[300]

Sovereigns were sold from 1943 onward to preserve the currency as a source of seigniorage. Greek administrators knew there was a connexion

Table 8.1. Private gold stocks in Greece, 1941-46.

Pre-war private gold stocks	3.1
German gold imports	1.2
British gold imports for partisans	0.7
1945 drachma support	0.15
Official gold sales in 1946	2.1
Total gold in private hands, end 1946	7.25

between the gold-exchange rate and the domestic price level, so gold-exchange rate operations became the panacea for monetary ailments. In a way, they were a substitute for monetary policy. Holding depreciating drachmas could not furnish business with working capital so business tried to hold its turnover capital and savings either as gold or as merchandise. If prices soared, then, in the absence of gold, business would try to increase its inventories of merchandise, for this was the only available stable asset. That meant bidding to buy stock for drachmas, and raising selling prices to defend this stock against purchase by others, including the consumer. Politicians damned this response as "speculation" at the expense of the rest of society. In reality, it reflected the paucity of asset choices. If however, an increasing volume of gold became available as a surrogate form of liquidity, business could protect its working capital by buying gold. Experience in 1945 showed that gold was a sound investment whose value appreciated relative to merchandise. When new supplies of gold were released, the exchange rate would steady. Businessmen would then be less reluctant to sell off stock, because the drachmas earned could be reconverted into gold. So gold sales tended to cause inventory releases, easing merchandise supply, raising mass purchasing power, and slowing inflation.

The authorities may not have understood the mechanism, but they knew it worked. Herman Neubacher spent this period incarcerated in a Yugoslav gaol, but the financing techniques he introduced in Greece during the occupation continued to provide the guiding spirit for the financial (mis)government of the country.

As official gold sales were inexorably associated in the official mind with "speculation," the authorities affected to find their own gold sales policy repugnant. Mantzavinos, as Governor of the Bank of Greece following Varvaressos' departure, asked (rhetorically) in the Bank's first post-war annual report whether the Bank's "policy of securing monetary stability ... by disposal of foreign exchange and gold ... [was] correct." Admitting to doubts, he was "nevertheless convinced that the monetary policy applied" had avoided economic collapse. But "we cannot ... pass in silence the disastrous tactics of the transactions in gold coins." This "unwholesome habit," an "oppressive remnant of the ... inflation of the enemy occupation ..." undermined public confidence in the drachma, and was a "crime against the country's economy." The "tendency to invest in gold coins was followed by ... those who succeeded in realising easy and big profits." [301]

The more gold entered into circulation, the larger its role would become as an alternative currency, i.e. an alternative to holding and exchanging drachma denominated financial claims. Makinen accounts for the exceptional pace of the Greek inflation in 1944 in terms of the displacement of the drachma by the sovereign. Increased availability of sovereigns would, in theory, reduce the need of the public to hold drachmas, narrowing the base for inflation tax, pressing up the rate of note issue and inflation needed to maintain a constant stream of real resources.[302] However, gold sales were specifically undertaken to preserve the monetary characteristics of the drachma, not to undermine them, and to a significant extent they achieved that end. The real choice for asset holders in the absence of a gold sales policy was between drachmas and merchandise. As drachmas could not be held as a store of value, then in the absence of a gold alternative, business would protect its assets by hoarding commodities. This merely speeded up inflation. The escape route into gold made possible the dis-hoarding of merchandise in late 1944, and the consequent revival of real wages. It did so again in 1946.

However gold, the alternative currency of choice, was inefficient as an alternative to stable money deposits, since there existed no gold or gold-linked credit base. Mantzavinos thought gold hoarding deprived the banks of the drachma funds which should have flowed to them as deposits, and prevented them from furnishing business with credits. He felt "sure that if those suffering from the disease of the gold mania were conscious of the harm caused by them to the country and if they discerned the losses which they will sustain from the investment of their money in gold coins, they would prefer productive investments to speculation in gold."[303] This was absurdly unrealistic. The return on deposits was massively negative in real terms, so gold holding was no "disease." It was virtually the only way a wealth holder could protect the value of his liquid assets. Yet Patterson notes that "even in private conversation with the foreign members of the Currency Committee [i.e. with himself and Sir John Nixon] the Greek officials were most reluctant to acknowledge that the demand for gold was due to more basic financial and economic factors than the operations of speculators."[304]

London only sanctioned the gold sales policy to buy the time needed to put the fiscal fundamentals in order. However, as gold sales also provided a viable alternative to fiscal reform, the time bought was not effectively used. Rather they protracted the period during which the authorities could earn seigniorage from printing drachmas.

There is of course a paradox. Without the stabilisation programmes for which they demonstrated so little enthusiasm, the post-liberation Greek authorities could not have continued to finance the state with seigniorage. This paradox is easily explained. They were only opposed to stabilizations because the foreign advisers told them that stabilisation required them to balance the budget, so they were obliged to make commitments which they invariably had to repudiate. Yet the policies pursued in 1943 and 1944 by the Axis administrators showed they could secure enough price stability to carry on printing money by intervening in the currency market with sales of gold or foreign exchange, without instituting fiscal reforms. Such sales would deplete gold stocks, but this did not matter to the liberation politicians, for financial crises would frighten their allies into putting up more cash.[305] Eventually, in 1946 and 1947, they got their way, more or less, so their attitude was less irrational than it seemed to the foreign advisers.

Gold sales therefore explain to a significant extent the long duration of the hyperinflation, because they preserved the drachma as a source of seigniorage. In this respect, the Greek experience differs from that of Hungary in 1946 and Yugoslavia in 1989 and 1992-1994. In both of these cases, governments, so far from having foreign exchange at their disposal, were eager to squeeze domestic hoards of hard currency from the hands of their hard-pressed citizens. (In neither case was the option open, as it was to Germany in the incipient stages of its hyperinflation, of dumping inflation currency on the international market). Internal currency dumping in both Hungary in 1946 and in Yugoslavia (in 1989 and in 1992-4) was pursued on a grand scale, especially to build up exchange reserves and merchandise inventories in advance of prospective stabilizations. This action had the analogous but reverse effect of official gold sales in Greece. It rapidly accelerated inflation, and shrank the tax-base for seigniorage, precipitating the need for currency reform, cosmetic or otherwise. The tactic, though morally unedifying, also made these currency reforms easier to implement. Currency dumping, by accelerating inflation, depressed popular purchasing power. This forced more and more foreign exchange holders to part with their hoards to just maintain a minimal living standard. It also dragged real wages down so low as to make it easy to win public acceptance of hardship wages after stabilisation.[306] In Greece, gold-sale policies supported relatively high real wages during pre-stabilisation crises, leading to acute resistance to austere wage setting in the post-stabilisation periods. Moreover, they established an unsustainably high real wage norm for the civil service, and this made it harder than ever to balance the budget.

The initial effect on the economy of the 1946 gold sales programme was merely to facilitate the accumulation of "idle" balances. Business was cautious about investing in reconstruction. Patterson criticised the authorities (and their British advisers) for refusing to let the banks operate stable value savings accounts. However, he thought that the overwhelming preference by Greeks for holding gold over all other assets, real as well as financial, resulted from the expectation on the part of the more affluent that the country would fall to the Communists.[307]

From the Whitehall perspective, the absorption of official gold into private portfolios was tantamount to throwing it down the drain. Official dogma post-war held that internationally negotiable values should stand only at the disposition of governments. In the short run, the retention of gold in "idle" hoards seems to justify this view. In the longer run, however, business was building up liquidity which could finance economic expansion under more auspicious circumstances. When news broke of the United States commitment to Greece in March 1947, businessmen expected the Americans would save Greece from Communism, and that US financial assistance would re-stabilise the drachma. Large quantities of sovereigns were sold back to the Bank of Greece, since the restoration of confidence caused businessmen to reduce their preference for liquidity and to seek funds for industrial investment.[308] Moreover, the economy was beginning to recover rapidly. Real national income rose 62 percent between 1945 and 1946, without the need for much new investment, since the main need was to reactivate existing sources of production. Thereafter, economic recovery and growth would require more investment, and now the hard currency liquidity disposed by business would provide access to the capital imports it needed to sustain expansion.

I conclude on a pessimistic note. Till I had looked more deeply into the historical economics of hyperinflation, I believed it to be the ultimate sanction against fiscal recklessness, a disease which finally forced a return to prudent financing. The cases of Sargent's four big inflations seemed to bear this out. Their longest lasting outcome had been to fix in the mind of governments and the public an inter-generational fear of the consequences of resorting to the printing press. Yet Hungary was destined to hyperinflate twice. Greece was to use the inflation machine as a political ploy in its uneasy dependency relationship with its foreign protectors, and to reap no small benefit from this. More recently, the periodic bouts of wild inflation in Russia and Yugoslavia and the foreign responses to them have suggested that governments learn quickly that hyperinflation can be switched off by largely cosmetic reforms which avoid disturbing existing structures. Both the reforms themselves and the subsequent resurgence of inflation when they fail can be deployed to justify further appeals for foreign macroeconomic assistance. In the well chosen words of Mr. N. Carver, a student in my class on hyperinflation, "What creates the moral hazard is the use of foreign aid as a substitute for fiscal reform in the knowledge that domestic political stability has a foreign price." I could not put it better.

APPENDIX
Monthly inflation variables, 1941-46

The price level (table A1)

Our source series for prices measure the rent-inclusive cost of living in the Athens-Piraeus area. Up to March 1941, we have used the Bank of Greece cost of living index as reproduced by Delivanis and Cleveland, which was set at 100 for the 1 Sep. 1938 - 31 Aug. 1939 average. This index indicates that the cost of living in 1940, to which all our data have been standardised, was 11 percent above 1939.[309]

This series stops at March 1941, and for April 1941 - December 1945 we have used the Agapitides-Pizanias series for the cost of a "basket" representing a rent inclusive austerity budget (similarly covering the Athens - Piraeus area). This takes 1940 as its base line.[310] The index, designed to monitor real wages, was based up to November 1942 on a combination of fixed and black market goods prices, and thereafter on free market prices. The Agapitides series appears to be an arithmetical average of prices collected over each month as a whole, and is consequently distorted because "the average of prices is affected by the big numbers on the last days of the month."[311] For most months, therefore, the Agapitides index figure will be higher than the geometric mean price level, or the price level at mid month, but it cannot be corrected for this. (A test of the assumption that the index is an arithmetical average of prices at the beginning and end of each month produced unrealistic results, because of the irregularity of day to day price trends). An alternative index in Delivanis-Cleveland uses figures issued by the (Greek) Economic Council. This takes 1940 at 100, and extends to 10 November 1944, the day before the 50 billion to 1 re-denomination of the drachma carried out by the British and Greek authorities. This index does not diverge greatly from that of Agapitides up to October 1944. However, the Agapitides index has been employed in our calculation, because the data accompanying it enable its dis-aggregation, and therefore elimination of the house-rent component. (See below).

On 11 November 1944, the currency was re-denominated. The Bank of Greece cost of living index re-starts in re-denominated drachmas in November 1944, and is linked to prices in 1936-40. No figure is given for December, but the serial provides regular information from January 1945 onwards, from which month it is applied in our own composite serial, on the basis of its own 1940 linkage.

The re-denomination of the drachma to 50 billion to 1 was carried out in order to re-establish roughly the same (administered) exchange rate between the (new) drachma and the pound sterling as had pertained pre-war. According to an index compiled by the Joint Relief Committee, the cost of living in new drachmas on re-denomination day, 11 November 1944, was 3.8 times that of 1939.[312]

The cost-of living indexes understate the rise in the price level, mainly because of the inclusion of house rent, which was tightly controlled. To create a better price inflation measure, we have reconstructed a rent-excluded index. In the Agapitides index, the value of the basket in 1940 was 3,745 drachmas, of which 1,200 drachmas was allocated for rent. Agapitides' tables also gave six-monthly (October and April) price breakdowns of the cost of living components. For intermediate months, we have interpolated rent charges. Our rent exclusive index subtracts rent charges (base year rent times the rent index) from the cash value of the basket. The error caused by interpolating rent data is negligible, because up to April 1942, rents were frozen, and fell in real terms to 1.7 percent of 1940. By this time rent comprised only 0.8 percent of the basket, and although rent was subsequently revised upward from time to time, its fraction of the basket was never to exceed 1.4 percent of pre-war.

On re-denomination, house rents were reset at 50 percent of their pre-war nominal level, which meant that they ceased to be negligible. They were raised to 75 percent in March 1945, 100 percent in July, 300 percent in December, 800 percent in February 1946, and 1200 percent in July - December that year. In the Bank of Greece index, rent was allocated 14.9 percent of the cost of living basket of 1939, when the basket itself cost 6,751 drachmas. On this basis, the rent-excluded cost of living index for 1945 and 1946 is calculated as for the period covered by the Agapitides index.

The resultant composite rent-excluded cost of living index, expressed throughout in "old" drachmas, is used as our proxy for prices in the text, and as a deflator in all calculations which express values in 1940 drachmas, except real wages, for which we apply the rent-inclusive figure. It still slightly understates the movement of free market prices because it includes administered, and artificially low utilities prices.

In addition to these monthly "average" prices, it was also useful to include a point-reference price for re-denomination day, 11 November 1944. For this we have used the cost of living (rent included) calculation of the Joint Relief committee for that day, of 3.8 in re-denominated drachmas, where 1939=1. This figure substantially exceeds Agapitides' November "average," presumably because of the sharp deceleration of the inflation rate after re-denomination.

Cagan's calculations for the Greek hyper-inflation used the Delivanis-Cleveland cost of living. From this he took hyper-inflation as beginning in October 1943 and ending in November 1944. However, using Cagan's hyper-inflation criteria, and our revised rent-excluded index, hyper-inflation began in June 1941, and ended in January 1946. Inflation exceeded 50 percent per month in June, July and November 1941, stayed below 50 percent in December 1941 to September 1942, exceeded it in October, and after eleven months of lower inflation, hit 66.2 percent in October 1943. The most intense inflation period extended to December 1944, but inflation exceeded 50 percent each month between October 1945 and January 1946. As Cagan's definition of the ending of a hyper-inflation requires that price increases should fall below 50 percent a month for a least a year, the hyper-inflation which began in June 1941 only ceased in February 1946.

The gold exchange rate of the drachma (table A2)

The market price of the sovereign in drachmas is taken from Agapitides-Pizanias, p. 17, for 1940 and January 1941 to December 1944. For January 1945 to March 46: it is taken from *Minaion statistikon deltion* Nov. 1946, table 24, and for April - December 1946 from the Delivanis and Cleveland appendix. These also appear to be monthly arithmetic averages.

Unlike Makinen, I do not treat the sovereign price in this study as a superior proxy to the Agapitides and Bank of Greece series for prices, firstly because excluding rent from these price series greatly improves their usefulness and secondly because of the use of gold sales as a means of depressing inflation. The gold price should be used exactly as the authorities viewed it - as a market exchange rate, and a lead indicator of domestic inflation.

The money supply, M0 and M1 (table A3)

Most of our figures for end of month circulation of Bank of Greece notes up to December 1943 are derived from an index in Delivanis and Cleveland. To convert the index data into absolute figures, this index was linked to Hahn's figure of 3,945 billion drachmas at end January 1944, which is extremely close to the British intelligence figure of 3,942 million in the same month. For end January - end August 1944, our figures are from Hahn. For September 1944, our estimate is Delivanis-Cleveland's index figure, linked to their January 1944 index figure, and Hahn's absolute figure for January.

For April and May 1941, Delivanis and Cleveland supply no data, so Hahn's round figure estimate of 21 billion drachmas for April was substituted, and May 1941's figure is interpolated between this figure and that based on the Delivanis-Cleveland index for June. For 31 October 1944, and 10 Nov. 1944, we have used Patterson's circulation figures.[313]

Anderson, Bomberger and Makinen prefer to use Agapitides series for note issue over that of Delivanis and Cleveland. In the latter months of the occupation, when inflation was at its most extreme, the Delivanis-Cleveland note issue races ahead of the Agapitides figure, from which Anderson et al. speculate that the former included stocks of as yet uncirculated notes on hand at its offices, whereas the latter included only those actually out in circulation.[314] There is a simpler explanation. Delivanis and Cleveland's index, like Hahn's absolute data, relate to end of month note issue volume, while Agapitides indexes issues as of the 15th of each month.[315] Where the end of month figure is more convenient to our analysis, we adhere to the use of the Hahn figures, substituting Delivanis and Cleveland where appropriate. Anderson et al may well be right that the series include uncirculated money, so *accidentally* the mid-month Agapitides figures could approximate more closely than those of Delivanis-Cleveland to the actuality of end-of month circulation, but such an assumption can hardly be harnessed for analytical purposes.[316]

Bank of Greece official figures for end of month circulation of new re-denominated notes are used for 11 November 1944 and from January 1945 - March 1946.[317]. For April-December 1946 the same figure is taken from Patterson as also are data for 30 November and end December 1944 (actually 1 Jan 1945).[318]

To calculate M1, we added to M0 sight deposits at the major banks. Intermittent figures for these deposits up to December 1943 are taken from a British intelligence report.[319] By then, deposits had sunk in value to less than 10 percent of M0. These figures are supplemented by data on deposits in Hahn (expressed as a percentage of M0) for October and December 1942 and February 1943.[320] Data for intermediate months for which data is lacking are interpolated geometrically. For the rest of the period up to re-denomination we assume the December 1943 deposits figure to remain unchanged, and therefore in real terms to have become negligible. (Deposits were only rising very slowly in the wildly inflationary months preceding this). Bank of Greece figures for sight deposits reappear from February 1945, when they totalled about one percent of M0.[321] It is assumed that between November 1944 and January 1945, their value was zero. For figures for July 1946 onwards, we have used Patterson's figures for "sight, savings and term deposits."[322] Patterson indicates that in March 1947, 85 percent of deposits of this type were sight deposits.

Seigniorage was calculated (in current prices) as the increment in M1 between the end of a given month and the end of the preceding month. The monthly volume of seigniorage in constant purchasing power has been calculated by deflating the increment in M1 by the geometric mean of the current and previous month's prices.

Occupation costs, Aug. 1941-Oct. 1944 (table A4)

Between April and the end of July 1941, the Axis occupation armies issued their own military scrip to meet local payments. In August 1941 however, these issues ceased, and till the end of the Occupation (October 1944) costs were paid by the Greek government to the German (and till September 1943, Italian) occupation authorities in drachmas from special occupation accounts at the Bank of Greece.

For August 1941 to July 1942, a table of monthly occupation payments to each of the occupiers is provided by Xydis.[323] These cross-check well with Hahn's quarterly data for payments to Germany, so are treated as reliable. Additionally, total occupation costs for September 1942 are given as 23 billion drachmas, and for September 1943 as 104 billion drachmas. (National Bank of Greece, *Reports* ... , p. 40). Italy announced its surrender on 8 September 1943 and we have assumed in our calculation that after that date, all further occupation costs were paid to the Germans.

German occupation costs. The Xydis figures for the period up to July 1942 are used for German occupation costs. A table in Hahn shows a cumulative total of payments by the Bank of Greece for German occupation costs, on a quarterly basis till the end of 1943, thereafter monthly.[324] Where possible the quarterly figures have been substituted with monthly data. According to Hahn, (German) occupation costs were 20.2 billion drachmas in October 1942, 4.75 billion in December, 20 billion a month in January - March 1943,[325] 30 billion in May 1943 and 440 billion in December that year.[326] We estimate German occupation costs in September 1943 at the total 104 billion cited by the National Bank of Greece,[327] and deduct our estimate for Italian costs during the same month. Since the Axis occupiers calculated the levy in terms of the sovereign rate on the drachma, we have converted known drachma payments into sovereign equivalents, using the gold index above. Exceptionally for October 1944, we have substituted Agapitides' sovereign exchange rate by the much lower estimated rate provided by Hahn (80 billion drachmas) since the latter probably relates only to the early part of the month, when Greece was still under German occupation.

We have interpolated German occupation costs in August and September 1942, April and June to August, October and November 1943, on the principle that the value of occupation costs in sovereigns was equal during sequential months which are covered only by quarterly figures. These monthly figures have then been re-converted into current drachmas.

Italian occupation costs are given by Xydis to July 1942, who also gives total occupation costs in March 1943, (35 billion drachmas) from which German costs are subtracted. Similarly, German costs are subtracted from the National Bank figure for September 1942. For August 1942 and October 1942-February 1943, for which we lack data, we have taken the Bank of Greece figure for total occupation costs April 1942 - March 1943, 290.8 billion drachmas,[328] subtracted from this payments to Germany and known payments to Italy, then averaged out the drachma payments in the months for which data is lacking, in terms of a constant gold-equivalent sum (£58,780 gold) per month. For April-8 September 1943, we have taken the Bank of Greece estimated payment to Italy of £2,213,954, subtracted from this the gold value of all payments made to Italy up to March 1943, and apportioned the rest per month pro-rata,

115

(i.e. £187,309 gold per month and £50,011 in early September). German, Italian and total monthly occupation costs are tabulated in gold and in current drachmas.

From December 1943 to the first week in October 1944 the Germans financed part of their occupation costs indirectly by selling sovereigns and gold francs for drachmas on the Athens stock exchange. The proceeds were spent in Greece, and augmented the sums raised from the occupation levies. Hahn provides a table of these sales, expressed as a percentage of the occupation costs financed by the Greek authorities.[329]

Table A5 then recalculates M1, the creation of new money (seigniorage), occupation payments, seigniorage received by the Greek government (seigniorage less occupation payments) and monthly change in M1, all in terms of 1940 drachmas. The data in this table are condensed into our text table 2.1 for the government accounts according to fiscal years (April-March) during the occupation period. For government spending, revenue and deficits after the liberation, we reproduce the monthly figures for government payments and receipts through the Bank of Greece, and their equivalent in 1940 drachmas.

Real wages (tables A6 and A7)

Table A6 and Figure 3 (i) show real wage trends in Greece from 1940 to the end of 1945. The table uses Agapitides' monthly index for civil service salaries, the salaries for private employees and the day wage for unskilled workers. The 1940 base values for this index were given in the same report as follows:

> Actual wage, 1940:
> Civil servant (month) 3800 dr.
> Private employee. (month) 4000 dr.
> Labourers (day) 58 dr., assuming a work-month of 26 days.

The wages and salaries indexes are converted to current drachmas. They were then deflated by the rent inclusive cost of living. Post-war, government salaries were paid 1/2 month in advance.[330] This appears also to have been the practice at least at the Bank of Greece before the war, and for paying civil servants during the occupation.[331] We assume therefore that recipients of Government salaries for any given month faced prices as of the 1st of the month - i.e. the price level of the preceding month multiplied by the mean of current month. It does not appear that any such concession was accorded in the private sector.

In the private sector, we take payment of wages as occurring every 10th day to end August 1944, later every 5th day. Therefore pay is deflated up to August by prices at the 10th of the month and for Sep. 44-Nov. 44, by the index as of the 5th of the month. Onto the basic wage rates shown by this source are added the value in 1940 drachmas of compulsory wage supplements from February 1944, as given in Delivanis and Cleveland, p. 93. The value of the wage in kind is taken as its value at moment of wage payment.

In table A7, a general index for monthly wages and salaries from the liberation onwards, based on October 1940=100, was provided by Patterson (pp. 122, 431). For civil service salaries during the same period, we have used data in Delivanis and Cleveland.[332]

Table A1. Conversion of rent inclusive cost of

month	rent inclusive austerity basket: (Agapitides) source 1	Agapitides rent index source 2	Agapitides basket, indexed to exclude rent (index)	rent inclusive B of G c of l index source 3	rent inclusive B of G c of l index source 4	ditto 1940=1
1938					100	0.910
1939					99	0.901
1940	3745	1	1.000		109.9	1.000
Aug-39	-	1		99		0.892
Sep-39	-	1		100		0.901
Oct-39	-	1		100		0.901
Nov-39	-	1		100		0.901
Dec-39	-	1		101		0.910
Jan-40	-	1		104		0.937
Feb-40	-	1		104		0.937
Mar-40	-	1		106		0.955
Apr-40	-	1		107		0.964
May-40	-	1		110		0.991
Jun-40	-	1		111		1.000
Jul-40	-	1		111		1.000
Aug-40	-	1		112		1.009
Sep-40	-	1		114		1.027
Oct-40	-	1		115		1.036
Nov-40	-	1		118		1.063
Dec-40	-	1		120		1.081
Jan-41	3956	1	1.083	125		1.126
Feb-41	3971	1	1.089	126		1.135
Mar-41	4133	1	1.152	128		1.153
Apr-41	4250	1	1.198			
May-41	5332	1	1.624			
Jun-41	7495	1	2.473			
Jul-41	11965	1	4.230			
Aug-41	15185	1	5.495			
Sep-41	21249	1	7.878			
Oct-41	28365	1	10.67			
Nov-41	46623	1	17.85			
Dec-41	60513	1	23.31			

living series to standardized consumer prices

B of G rent index source 5	B of G c of l excl. rent	General index of c of l excl. rent	General index of c of l incl. rent	Monthly inflation rate(%) (c of l, excl. rent)	month
1					1938
1	0.885	0.885	0.901		1939
1	1.000	1.000	1.000		1940
1	0.875	0.875	0.892	-	Aug-39
1	0.886	0.886	0.901	1.2	Sep-39
1	0.886	0.886	0.901	0.0	Oct-39
1	0.886	0.886	0.901	0.0	Nov-39
1	0.896	0.896	0.910	1.2	Dec-39
1	0.927	0.927	0.937	3.5	Jan-40
1	0.927	0.927	0.937	0.0	Feb-40
1	0.948	0.948	0.955	2.2	Mar-40
1	0.958	0.958	0.964	1.1	Apr-40
1	0.990	0.990	0.991	3.3	May-40
1	1.000	1.000	1.000	1.1	Jun-40
1	1.000	1.000	1.000	0.0	Jul-40
1	1.010	1.010	1.009	1.0	Aug-40
1	1.031	1.031	1.027	2.1	Sep-40
1	1.042	1.042	1.036	1.0	Oct-40
1	1.073	1.073	1.063	3.0	Nov-40
1	1.094	1.094	1.081	1.9	Dec-40
1	1.146	1.146	1.056	4.8	Jan-41
1	1.156	1.156	1.060	0.9	Feb-41
1	1.177	1.177	1.104	1.8	Mar-41
		1.198	1.135	1.8	Apr-41
		1.624	1.424	35.5	May-41
		2.473	2.001	52.3	Jun-41
		4.230	3.195	71.0	Jul-41
		5.495	4.055	29.9	Aug-41
		7.878	5.674	43.4	Sep-41
		10.67	7.574	35.5	Oct-41
		17.85	12.45	67.2	Nov-41
		23.31	16.16	30.6	Dec-41

table A1 continued

month	rent inclusive austerity basket: (Agapitides) source 1	Agapitides rent index source 2	Agapitides basket, indexed to exclude rent (index)	rent inclusive B of G c of l index source 3	rent inclusive B of G c of l index source 4	ditto 1940=1
Jan-42	70478	1	27.22			
Feb-42	98133	1	38.09			
Mar-42	111195	1	43.22			
Apr-42	151919	1	59.22			
May-42	173307	1	67.63			
Jun-42	218875	1	85.53			
Jul-42	225499	1	88.13			
Aug-42	326673	1	127.9			
Sep-42	366343	1	143.5			
Oct-42	583848	2	228.5			
Nov-42	476102	2	186.1			
Dec-42	333590	2	130.1			
Jan-43	339826	2	132.6			
Feb-43	304293	2	118.6			
Mar-43	340142	2	132.7			
Apr-43	436460	3	170.1			
May-43	418502	3	163.0			
Jun-43	457170	3	178.2			
Jul-43	547950	3	213.9			
Aug-43	684055	3	267.4			
Sep-43	791816	3	309.7			
Oct-43	1327821	15	514.7			
Nov-43	2371162	15	924.6			
Dec-43	3102640	15	1212			
Jan-44	7919413	15	3105			
Feb-44	11429445	15	4484			
Mar-44	32185465	15	12639			
Apr-44	44245747	100	17338			
May-44	115020008	100	45147			
Jun-44	281696667	100	110639			
Jul-44	621496118	100	244156			
Aug-44	3.941E+09	100	1548398			
Sep-44	7.948E+10	100	31229105			

B of G rent index source 5	B of G c of l excl. rent	General index of c of l excl. rent	General index of c of l incl. rent	Monthly inflation rate(%) (c of l, excl. rent)	month
		27.22	18.82	16.8	Jan-42
		38.09	26.20	39.9	Feb-42
		43.22	29.69	13.5	Mar-42
		59.22	40.57	37.0	Apr-42
		67.63	46.28	14.2	May-42
		85.53	58.44	26.5	Jun-42
		88.13	60.21	3.0	Jul-42
		127.9	87.23	45.1	Aug-42
		143.5	97.82	12.2	Sep-42
		228.5	155.9	59.2	Oct-42
		186.1	127.1	-18.5	Nov-42
		130.1	89.08	-30.1	Dec-42
		132.6	90.74	1.9	Jan-43
		118.6	81.25	-10.5	Feb-43
		132.7	90.83	11.9	Mar-43
		170.1	116.5	28.2	Apr-43
		163.0	111.7	-4.1	May-43
		178.2	122.1	9.3	Jun-43
		213.9	146.3	20.0	Jul-43
		267.4	182.7	25.0	Aug-43
		309.7	211.4	15.8	Sep-43
		514.7	354.6	66.2	Oct-43
		924.6	633.2	79.7	Nov-43
		1212	828.5	31.1	Dec-43
		3105	2115	156.2	Jan-44
		4484	3052	44.4	Feb-44
		12639	8594	181.9	Mar-44
		17338	11815	37.2	Apr-44
		45147	30713	160.4	May-44
		110639	75219	145.1	Jun-44
		244156	165954	120.7	Jul-44
		1548398	1052281	534.2	Aug-44
		31229105	21222481	1916.9	Sep-44

table A1 continued

month	rent inclusive austerity basket: (Agapitides) source 1	Agapitides rent index source 2	Agapitides basket, indexed to exclude rent (index)	rent inclusive B of G c of l index source 3	rent inclusive B of G c of l index source 4	ditto 1940=1
Oct-44	6.008E+12	20000	2.361E+09			
Nov-44	2.832E+14	20000	1.113E+11		394.6	3.591
Dec-44	2.048E+15	2.5E+10	7.931E+11		-	
Jan-45				827.7		7.531
Feb-45					699.5	6.365
Mar-45					609.7	5.548
Apr-45					808.5	7.357
May-45					1126.0	10.246
Jun-45					1169.1	10.638
Jul-45					1066.3	9.702
Aug-45					1079.7	9.824
Sep-45					1562.3	14.216
Oct-45					2459.8	22.382
Nov-45					3917.4	35.645
Dec-45					7422.7	67.540
Jan-46					15822.1	143.968
Feb-46					13662.2	124.315
Mar-46					13955.1	126.980
Apr-46					14251.3	129.675
May-46					14426.1	131.266
Jun-46					14459.4	131.569
Jul-46					14418.1	131.193
Aug-46					13979.2	127.199
Sep-46					14435.7	131.353
Oct-46					14879.1	135.388
Nov-46					15431.3	140.412
Dec-46					14550.1	132.394
10 November 1944 (note 1)						
	7.059E+14	20000	2.774E+11			
11 November 1944 (note 2)						
					3.8	3.42311
						3.59054

B of G rent index source 5	B of G c of l excl. rent	General index of c of l excl. rent	General index of c of l incl. rent	Monthly inflation rate(%) (c of l, excl. rent)	month
		2.361E+09	1.604E+09	7458.7	Oct-44
0.5	4.070	1.113E+11	7.562E+10	4614.1	Nov-44
0.5		7.931E+11	5.470E+11	612.7	Dec-44
0.5	8.621	4.311E+11	3.766E+11	-45.6	Jan-45
0.5	7.274	3.637E+11	3.182E+11	-15.6	Feb-45
0.75	6.292	3.146E+11	2.774E+11	-13.5	Mar-45
0.75	8.381	4.190E+11	3.678E+11	33.2	Apr-45
0.75	11.718	5.859E+11	5.123E+11	39.8	May-45
0.75	12.171	6.085E+11	5.319E+11	3.9	Jun-45
1	11.052	5.526E+11	4.851E+11	-9.2	Jul-45
1	11.192	5.596E+11	4.912E+11	1.3	Aug-45
1	16.264	8.132E+11	7.108E+11	45.3	Sep-45
1	25.697	1.285E+12	1.119E+12	58.0	Oct-45
1	41.016	2.051E+12	1.782E+12	59.6	Nov-45
3	77.546	3.877E+12	3.377E+12	89.1	Dec-45
3	165.823	8.291E+12	7.198E+12	113.8	Jan-46
8	142.347	7.117E+12	6.216E+12	-14.2	Feb-46
8	145.426	7.271E+12	6.349E+12	2.2	Mar-46
8	148.539	7.427E+12	6.484E+12	2.1	Apr-46
8	150.376	7.519E+12	6.563E+12	1.2	May-46
8	150.726	7.536E+12	6.578E+12	0.2	Jun-46
12	149.671	7.484E+12	6.560E+12	-0.7	Jul-46
12	145.059	7.253E+12	6.360E+12	-3.1	Aug-46
12	149.856	7.493E+12	6.568E+12	3.3	Sep-46
12	154.516	7.726E+12	6.769E+12	3.1	Oct-46
12	160.320	8.016E+12	7.021E+12	3.8	Nov-46
12	151.059	7.553E+12	6.620E+12	-5.8	Dec-46
				10 November 1944 (note 1)	
		2.774E+11	1.885E+11		
				11 November 1944 (note 2)	
		2.035E+11	1.795E+11		

Notes to Table A1

Constants
1940 average of Bank of Greece cost of living (rent inclusive) index: 111.
Revaluation, 11 Nov. 1944: $5 *10^{10}$ old drachmas for one new.
Rent, 1940 (Agapitides) 1200 drachmas. (source 6)
Rent, 1939, weighted 0.149 in Bank of Greece cost of living index (source 7)

Sources
1 Agapitides, "Inflation of the Cost of Living", p. 645
2 Ibid. p. 647.
3 Delivanis and Cleveland, *Greek Monetary Developments*, p. 175.
4 Bank of Greece, *Monthly Bulletin*, XIII-4. April 1948, p. 13.
5 Ibid., housing column.
6 Agapitides, " Inflation of the Cost of Living", p. 644.
7 Bank of Greece, *Monthly Bulletin*, November 1946, table 27.

note 1. The "Economic council cost of living index" based on 1940, (Delivanis and Cleveland, *Greek Monetary Developments,* p. 175- stood at 1.885×10^{11} on 10 November 1944. The rent excluded figure is calculated as for the Agapitides index.

note 2. The Joint Relief Committee cost of living index (1939=1) in Delivanis and Cleveland, *Greek Monetary Developments,* shows 11 November (in new drachmas) at 3.8, i.e. 3.423 when indexed to 1940, which is sufficiently close to the Bank of Greece index for November 1944 (3.59) for us to assume that the latter index related to the first day of stabilisation.

Table A2. The gold price and the index of consumer prices in gold

month	price of sovereign		c of l excl.rent (in drachma terms)	c of l excl.rent in gold
	old drachmas	new drachmas		
1940	1100		1	100.0
Jan-41	1250		1.146	100.8
Feb-41	1250		1.156	101.7
Mar-41	1400		1.177	92.5
Apr-41	1500		1.198	87.9
May-41	3800		1.624	47.0
Jun-41	5000		2.473	54.4
Jul-41	10500		4.230	44.3
Aug-41	11000		5.495	55.0
Sep-41	12900		7.878	67.2
Oct-41	21400		10.67	54.9
Nov-41	28500		17.85	68.9
Dec-41	21100		23.31	121.5
Jan-42	23500		27.22	127.4
Feb-42	28200		38.09	148.6
Mar-42	34600		43.22	137.4
Apr-42	49900		59.22	130.5
May-42	57600		67.63	129.1
Jun-42	78500		85.53	119.9
Jul-42	118100		88.13	82.1
Aug-42	196300		127.9	71.7
Sep-42	214400		143.5	73.6
Oct-42	360000		228.5	69.8
Nov-42	274000		186.1	74.7
Dec-42	146000		130.1	98.0
Jan-43	144000		132.6	101.3
Feb-43	134600		118.6	96.9
Mar-43	162040		132.7	90.1
Apr-43	172300		170.1	108.6
May-43	240560		163.0	74.5
Jun-43	312300		178.2	62.8
Jul-43	326800		213.9	72.0

table A2 (gold prices) continued

month	price of sovereign		c of l excl.rent (in drachma terms)	c of l excl.rent
	old drachmas	new drachmas		
Aug-43	369550		267.4	79.6
Sep-43	430570		309.7	79.1
Oct-43	774660		514.7	73.1
Nov-43	1286670		924.6	79.0
Dec-43	1531000		1212	87.1
Jan-44	3126500		3105	109.2
Feb-44	5468300		4484	90.2
Mar-44	1.500E+07		12639	92.7
Apr-44	3.758E+07		17338	50.7
May-44	1.007E+08		45147	49.3
Jun-44	1.255E+08		110639	97.0
Jul-44	3.750E+08		244156	71.6
Aug-44	2.536E+09		1548398	67.2
Sep-44	1.834E+10		3.123E+07	187.3
Oct-44	2.233E+12		2.361E+09	116.3
Nov-44	9.765E+13	2661	1.113E+11	125.4
Dec-44	1.990E+14	3980	7.931E+11	438.4
Jan-45	1.902E+14	3803	4.311E+11	249.4
Feb-45	2.362E+14	4723	3.637E+11	169.4
Mar-45	2.672E+14	5343	3.146E+11	129.5
Apr-45	4.104E+14	8208	4.190E+11	112.3
May-45	8.053E+14	16105	5.859E+11	80.0
Jun-45	6.686E+14	13372	6.085E+11	100.1
Jul-45	6.446E+14	12892	5.526E+11	94.3
Aug-45	8.790E+14	17579	5.596E+11	70.0
Sep-45	1.264E+15	25279	8.132E+11	70.8
Oct-45	1.904E+15	38087	1.285E+12	74.2
Nov-45	2.733E+15	54654	2.051E+12	82.6
Dec-45	5.206E+15	104125	3.877E+12	81.9
Jan-46	7.417E+15	148346	8.291E+12	123.0
Feb-46	7.085E+15	141708	7.117E+12	110.5
Mar-46	6.794E+15	135875	7.271E+12	117.7
Apr-46	6.800E+15	136000	7.427E+12	120.1
May-46	6.738E+15	134750	7.519E+12	122.8
Jun-46	6.849E+15	136982	7.536E+12	121.0

month	price of sovereign		c of l excl.rent (in drachma terms)	c of l excl.rent in gold
	old drachmas	new drachmas		
Jul-46	6.729E+15	134585	7.484E+12	122.3
Aug-46	6.748E+15	134962	7.253E+12	118.2
Sep-46	6.779E+15	135587	7.493E+12	121.6
Oct-46	6.785E+15	135696	7.726E+12	125.3
Nov-46	6.813E+15	136264	8.016E+12	129.4
Dec-46	6.811E+15	136212	7.553E+12	122.0

Gold price

11/44-3/46: Bank of Greece, *Monthly Statistical Bulletin*, Nov. 1946, table 24.
4-12/46: Delivanis and Cleveland, *Greek Monetary Developments*, appendix.

Table A3.

COLUMN	A	B	C	D
	note circulation end month Billion. dr. Hahn, B of G	ditto GHQ	note index end month D & C	composite note circulation Billion. dr.
Sep-39	11	11	139	
Oct-39			129	
Nov-39			122	
Dec-39	9.4		124	9.32
Jan-40			117	8.79
Feb-40			116	8.72
Mar-40		9	118	8.87
Apr-40			129	9.69
May-40			144	10.82
Jun-40		11	150	11.27
Jul-40			139	10.45
Aug-40	12.594		145	10.90
Sep-40		11	148	11.12
Oct-40			165	12.40
Nov-40			186	13.98
Dec-40		15	201	15.11
Jan-41			212	15.93
Feb-41			223	16.76
Mar-41		19	254	19.09
Apr-41	21		n.d.	21.00
May-41			n.d.	22.34
Jun-41	24		315	23.67
Jul-41			315	23.67
Aug-41			381	28.63
Sep-41	34		447	33.59
Oct-41			513	38.55
Nov-41		41	565	42.46
Dec-41	49		645	48.47
Jan-42		50	697	52.38
Feb-42			763	57.34

Money supply

E	F	G	H	COLUMN
sight deposits (* =interpolation)* GHQ	M1 (notes + sight deposits)	ditto 15th month	new money creation during month	
14				Sep-39
14 *				Oct-39
15 *				Nov-39
15				Dec-39
16 *	24			Jan-40
16 *	25		0.57	Feb-40
17	26		0.82	Mar-40
17 *	26		0.49	Apr-40
16 *	27		0.79	May-40
16	27		0.12	Jun-40
16 *	27		-0.50	Jul-40
17 *	28		0.78	Aug-40
17	28		0.57	Sep-40
18 *	30		2.01	Oct-40
19 *	32		2.34	Nov-40
19	34		1.93	Dec-40
20 *	36	35.77	1.69	Jan-41
21 *	38	37.42	1.73	Feb-41
22	41	40.66	3.27	Mar-41
21 *	42	41.59	1.05	Apr-41
20 *	43	42.38	0.51	May-41
20 *	43	43.70	0.54	Jun-41
19 *	42	42.81	-0.76	Jul-41
18 *	47	47.15	4.23	Aug-41
17 *	51	51.08	4.26	Sep-41
17 *	55	55.59	4.28	Oct-41
16	58	59.35	3.26	Nov-41
20 *	68	66.12	10.01	Dec-41
25	77	74.79	8.91	Jan-42
29 *	86	84.67	8.72	Feb-42

Table A3 (Money supply) continued

COLUMN	A	B	C	D
	note circulation end month Billion. dr. Hahn, B of G	ditto GHQ	note index end month D & C	composite note circulation Billion. dr.
Mar-42	68		895	67.26
Apr-42			1039	78.08
May-42			1210	90.93
Jun-42	110		1447	108.74
Jul-42		120	1737	130.54
Aug-42			2040	153.31
Sep-42	186	185	2447	183.89
Oct-42			3132	235.37
Nov-42			3816	286.77
Dec-42	335		4408	331.26
Jan-43	350	350	4842	363.88
Feb-43			5289	397.47
Mar-43	466	450	6132	460.82
Apr-43			7368	553.71
May-43			8187	615.25
Jun-43	713	712	9377	704.68
Jul-43		869	11438	859.57
Aug-43		1073	13975	1050
Sep-43	1302	1276	17128	1287
Oct-43		1770	22825	1715
Nov-43		2000	30315	2278
Dec-43	3114	2800	42095	3163
Jan-44	3945	3942	52495	3945
Feb-44	5217	5220	67996	5217
Mar-44	8068		101607	8068
Apr-44	18091		221565	18091
May-44	32668		411022	32668
Jun-44	68636		804382	68636
Jul-44	130336		1726000	130336
Aug-44	555459		7274000	555459
Sep-44	2300000		96120000	7223419
Oct-44	725000000		9.139E+09	725000000

E	F	G	H	COLUMN
sight deposits (* =interpolation)* GHQ	M1 (notes + sight deposits)	ditto 15th month	new money creation during month	
33 *	100	97.89	14.25	**Mar-42**
38 *	116	113.71	15.80	**Apr-42**
44 *	135	131.99	18.58	**May-42**
50 *	159	155.51	24.41	**Jun-42**
58	189	184.82	29.38	**Jul-42**
75 *	229	219.44	40.16	**Aug-42**
98	282	251.88	53.19	**Sep-42**
108	344	311.08	61.75	**Oct-42**
107 *	394	367.43	50.26	**Nov-42**
106	437	409.00	43.36	**Dec-42**
105	469	452.62	31.61	**Jan-43**
115	513	493.64	43.86	**Feb-43**
158	619	569.68	106	**Mar-43**
179 *	732	669.94	113	**Apr-43**
202 *	817	773.53	85	**May-43**
228	933	873.87	116	**Jun-43**
258	1118	1033	185	**Jul-43**
276	1326	1224	209	**Aug-43**
282	1569	1414	243	**Sep-43**
300	2015	1742	446	**Oct-43**
320 *	2598	2323	583	**Nov-43**
340 *	3503	2951	905	**Dec-43**
360 *	4305	3737	802	**Jan-44**
380 *	5597	4858	1292	**Feb-44**
400	8468	6684	2871	**Mar-44**
420 *	18511	13347	10043	**Apr-44**
440 *	33108	26369	14597	**May-44**
460 *	69096	45316	35988	**Jun-44**
480 *	130816	88029	61720	**Jul-44**
500 *	555959	234607	425143	**Aug-44**
520 *	7223939	1668818	6667980	**Sep-44**
540 *	725000540	29973120	717776601	**Oct-44**

Table A3 (Money supply) continued

COLUMN	A	B	C	D
	note circulation end month Billion. dr. Hahn, B of G	ditto GHQ	note index end month D & C	composite note circulation Billion. dr.
10/11/44	6.28E+09		8.263E+10	6.28E+09
11/11/44	0.156			
Nov-44	1.362			6.81E+10
Dec-44	2.2			1.1E+11
Jan-45	5.062			2.531E+11
Feb-45	9.016			4.508E+11
Mar-45	12.78			6.39E+11
Apr-45	21.09			1.055E+12
May-45	25.762			1.288E+12
Jun-45	30.26			1.513E+12
Jul-45	33.624			1.681E+12
Aug-45	38.109			1.905E+12
Sep-45	46.98			2.349E+12
Oct-45	61.669			3.083E+12
Nov-45	76.377			3.819E+12
Dec-45	104.083			5.204E+12
Jan-46	131.472			6.574E+12
Feb-46	218.645			1.093E+13
Mar-46	278.743			1.394E+13
Apr-46	363.5			1.818E+13
May-46	389.4			1.947E+13
Jun-46	412			2.06E+13
Jul-46	444.1			2.221E+13
Aug-46	495.9			2.48E+13
Sep-46	511.7			2.559E+13
Oct-46	505.3			2.527E+13
Nov-46	468			2.34E+13
Dec-46	537.5			2.688E+13

E	F	G	H	COLUMN
sight deposits (* =interpolation)* GHQ	M1 (notes + sight deposits)	ditto 15th month	new money creation during month	
540 *	6.28E+09			10/11/44
0 *	7.80E+09			11/11/44
0 *	6.81E+10	1.932E+10	6.737E+10	Nov-44
0 *	1.100+11	7.770E+10	4.190E+10	Dec-44
0 *	2.531E+11	1.669E+11	1.431E+11	Jan-45
0.090	4.553E+11	3.395E+11	2.022E+11	Feb-45
0.253	6.516E+11	5.447E+11	1.963E+11	Mar-45
0.661	1.088E+12	8.418E+11	4.359E+11	Apr-45
0.957	1.336E+12	1.205E+12	2.484E+11	May-45
1.557	1.591E+12	1.458E+12	2.549E+11	Jun-45
1.926	1.778E+12	1.682E+12	1.867E+11	Jul-45
2.667	2.039E+12	1.904E+12	2.613E+11	Aug-45
2.941	2.496E+12	2.256E+12	4.572E+11	Sep-45
3.268	3.247E+12	2.847E+12	7.508E+11	Oct-45
3.807	4.009E+12	3.608E+12	7.623E+11	Nov-45
4.546	5.431E+12	4.666E+12	1.422E+12	Dec-45
5.901	6.869E+12	6.108E+12	1.437E+12	Jan-46
12.167	1.154E+13	8.903E+12	4.672E+12	Feb-46
16.139	1.474E+13	1.304E+13	3.204E+12	Mar-46
22.5	1.930E+13	1.687E+13	4.556E+12	Apr-46
30.7	2.101E+13	2.013E+13	1.705E+12	May-46
32.4	2.222E+13	2.160E+13	1.215E+12	Jun-46
43.2	2.437E+13	2.327E+13	2.145E+12	Jul-46
49.9	2.729E+13	2.579E+13	2.925E+12	Aug-46
55.9	2.838E+13	2.783E+13	1.090E+12	Sep-46
64.1	2.847E+13	2.842E+13	9E+10	Oct-46
65.4	2.667E+13	2.756E+13	-1.8E+12	Nov-46
67.8	3.027E+13	2.841E+13	3.595E+12	Dec-46

Notes to Table A3

Col. B

Note circulation.
Data from Hahn are used in preference to British intelligence data, where figures are given for same period.
For 12/39 and 10/44, see Patterson, Thesis.
For 10/11/44 see Delivanis & Cleveland, *Greek Monetary Developments*, appendix.
For 11/11/44 and 31/1/45 -31/3/46: Bank of Greece, *Monthly Bulletin*, Nov. 1946, Table 3.
For 30/11/44 Patterson, Thesis, p. 70. For 31/12/44, 4/1/45 figure, Patterson, Thesis, p. 135.
Data in B of E. OV 80.22, fo. 145 indicates that old drachma notes were included in the circulation figure.

Col. C

GHQ circulation figure.

Col. F

Sight deposits at banks.
Source: PRO T160.1265.18214.014.1. GHQ.MEF-WO, 20 Apr. 1944.
For 31/12/39, Bank of Greece figure for private deposits. (The GHQ figure is a rounded 15,000 million.)
For Oct. and Dec. 1942, and Feb. 1943, we have used . data on deposits expressed as a percentage of primary money, from Hahn, *Die Griechische Währung*.
Sight deposits Mar. 1944: B of E. OV 80.21 fo. 18.
Private deposits, 31/12/39 and 28/2/45-30/3/46: Bank of Greece, table 9.

Col. G (primary money)

Basis is month end figure: we use Hahn, *Die Griechische Währung*, figures for 31/12/43-31/8/44 where indexing Delivanis and Cleveland, *Greek Monetary Developments*, to 1/44 gives close agreement.
We use Delivanis and Cleveland, *Greek Monetary Developments*, for 30 Sept. 1944, where they diverge and Hahn resorts to round figures.
We use the Delivanis and Cleveland index based on 1/44 for all data from June 1941 as correspondence with Hahn and GHQ is good.
We use Hahn, *Die Griechische Währung*, for April 1941, as the only available figure.
We use Patterson, Thesis, p. 28 for 31/10/44 and 10/11/44.

Col. H

Composite primary money, at 15th of the month.

Basis is Agapitides' note circulation index. This was then linked to end month composite circulation for July 1941, when there was little or no change in the note issue during the month. However,

for November 1944, we have reduced the Agapitides figure by a factor of 10 and for December 1944, by a factor of 100. As it stood, his purported growth of the note circulation between October and November of 6446 fold is unrealistic in relation to a price increase of 47 fold, as reported by Agapitides, and of 95 fold (to 10 November) as reported by Delivanis & Cleveland, *Greek Monetary Developments*.

Table A4. Greek occupatio[n]

COLUMN	B	C	D	E	F	G	H
month	drachma/gold £ rate. (Agapitides)	cumulative occupation payments to Germany, billion dr. (Hahn)	monthly occupation payment to Germany, billion dr.	estimated monthly occupation payment to Germany, £ gold	cumulative occupation payment billion dr.		
					to Germany	to Axis	to Italy
Aug-41	11000		2.50	227000	2.50		
Sep-41	12900	4	2.39	185581	4.89		
Oct-41	21400		2.05	95794	6.94		
Nov-41	28500		0.93	32456	7.87	25	17.1
Dec-41	21100	10	3.60	170758	11.47		
Jan-42	23500		4.40	187064	15.87	45	29.1
Feb-42	28200		4.59	162730	20.45		
Mar-42	34600	24	5.43	156936	25.88		
Apr-42	49900		6.71	134369	32.59		
May-42	57600		12.51	217118	45.10		
Jun-42	78500	58	14.72	187516	59.82		
Jul-42	118100		15.75	133362	75.57		
Aug-42	196300		14.94 *	76090	90.50		
Sep-42	214400	105	16.31 *	76090	106.8	170	63
Oct-42	360000		20.20	56111	127.0	196 *	69
Nov-42	274000		17.05	62226	144.1	226 *	82
Dec-42	146000	147	4.75	32534	148.8	260	11[?]
Jan-43	144000		20	138889	168.8	322 *	153
Feb-43	134600		20	148588	188.8	398	209
Mar-43	162040	207	20	123426	208.8	441	232
Apr-43	172300		21.4 *	124068	230.2	492 *	262
May-43	240560		30.0	124709	260.2	549 *	289
Jun-43	312300	300	41.6 *	133279	301.8	613	31[?]
Jul-43	326800		85.0 *	260001	386.8	757	370
Aug-43	369550		96.1 *	260001	482.9	939	456
Sep-43	430570	593	111.9 *	260001	594.8		
Oct-43	774660		175.1 *	226068	769.9		
Nov-43	1286670		290.9 *	226068	1061		
Dec-43	1531000	1499	440	287394	1501		
Jan-44	3126500	2209	710	227091	2211		
Feb-44	5468300	3489	1280	234076	3491		
Mar-44	15003000	6529	3040	202626	6531		

payments 1941-44

I	J	K	L	M	N	O	COLUMN
monthly occupation payments to Italy, billion dr.	estimated monthly payment to Italy, £ gold	estimated total payments, £ gold monthly	estimated total payments, billion dr. monthly	German gold sales (% of total payment)	German gold sales, £ gold	overall German spending, £ gold	month
1.50	136364	363364	4	-			Aug-41
1.50	116279	301860	4	-			Sep-41
0.50	23364	119159	3	-			Oct-41
0.75	26316	58772	2	-			Nov-41
3.34	158294	329052	7	-			Dec-41
1.03	43830	230894	5	-			Jan-42
1.20	42553	205284	6	-			Feb-42
1.30	37572	194509	7	-			Mar-42
1.75	35070	169439	8	-			Apr-42
1.75	30382	247500	14	-			May-42
5.95	75796	263312	21	-			Jun-42
2.97	25140	158501	19	-			Jul-42
4.46 *	22698	98787	19	-			Aug-42
6.69 ◆	31187	107276	23	-			Sep-42
5.67 ◆	15736	71848	26	-			Oct-42
12.75 ◆	46534	108761	30	-			Nov-42
29.58 ◆	202633	235168	34	-			Dec-42
41.68 ◆	289466	428355	62	-			Jan-43
56.32 ◆	418402	566991	76	-			Feb-43
23.00 ◆	141940	265367	43	-			Mar-43
29.79 ◆	172897	296965	51	-			Apr-43
27.10 ◆	112669	237378	57	-			May-43
22.11 ◆	70785	204064	64	-			Jun-43
59.03 ◆	180636	440636	144	-			Jul-43
85.92 ◆	232490	492491	182	-			Aug-43
-7.95 ◆	-18460	241540	104	3)	15000	256540	Sep-43
0	0	226068	175	3)	30000	256068	Oct-43
0	0	226068	291	3)	20000	246068	Nov-43
0	0	287394	440	0.16	54742	342136	Dec-43
0	0	227091	710	0.16	43255	270346	Jan-44
0	0	234076	1280	0.23	69919	303995	Feb-44
0	0	202626	3040	0.59	291584	494210	Mar-44

*= interpolation. ◆= derived from accumulated value.

137

Table A4 continued

COLUMN	B	C	D	E	F	G	H
month	drachma/gold £rate. (Agapitides)	cumulative occupation payments to Germany billion dr. (Hahn)	monthly occupation payment to Germany billion dr.	estimated monthly occupation payment to Germany £ gold	cumulative occupation payment billion d		
					to Germany	to Axis	to Italy
Apr-44	37583000	15429	8900	236809	15431		
May-44	100680000	28129	12700	126142	28131		
Jun-44	125460000	52129	24000	191296	52131		
Jul-44	374950000	99579	47450	126550	99581		
Aug-44	2.536E+09	345579	246000	96988	345581		
Sep-44	1.834E+10	1665947	1320368	71994	1665949		
Oct-44	8E+10	3465947	1800000	22500	3465949		
TOTALS				6042300			

I	J	K	L	M	N	O	COLUMN
monthly occupation payments to Italy billion dr.	estimated monthly payment to Italy £ gold	estimated total payments £ gold monthly	estimated total payments billion dr. monthly	German gold sales (% of total payment)	German gold sales £ gold	overall German spending £ gold	month
0	0	236809	8900	0.31	106393	343202	Apr-44
0	0	126142	12700	0.33	62130	188272	May-44
0	0	191296	24000	0.25	63765	255061	Jun-44
0	0	126550	47450	0.72	325415	451965	Jul-44
0	0	96988	246000	0.32	45641	142629	Aug-44
0	0	71994	1320368	0.24	22735	94729	Sep-44
0	0	22500	1800000	0.43	16974	39474	Oct-44
	2670573.4	8712873	3466368		1167552		**TOTALS**
total during gold action		2517142					

139

Notes to Table A4

1) 9/42: axis occupation expenses, given by National Bank of Greece, p. 40. 23 mrd. drachmas.

2) 4/42-3/43 total occupation expenditure, given by Bank of Greece, p. 102 = 290.8 mrd. drachmas.

3) See note to col. N.

4) Total occupation costs Sep. 1943 were (National Bank of Greece, p. 40) 104 billion drachmas.

Sources and notes

Col. B

Agapitides-Pizanias, p. 17.
Exception. October 1944. Hahn's gold-rate (8×10^{10} dr./ sovereign) is used in preference to Agapitides' since Hahn's rate relates only to the early part of the month while Greece was still occupied.

Col. C

Note: Cumulative occupation payments from Hahn, *Griechische Wahrung*, p.41 are payments to Germany only, since they roughly agree with monthly payments to Germany up to June 1942 (Col D) in Xydis, *Economy and Finances*, p. 44.

Col. D

German occupation payments to Jul. 42, from Xydis, , *Economy and Finances*, p.44. Oct. 42, Dec. 42 and Jan.-Mar. 1943: Hahn, *Griechische Wahrung*, p. 22; May 43, Dec. 43: Hahn, p. 28; Interpolations assume a constant gold value of monthly payments over the relevant quarter.
Jan 1944-Oct 1944: by subtraction from accumulated. totals in col. C.

Col. E

Col. D values of occupation payments to Germany, expressed in £ gold.
April 1943 value is interpolated between March and May.

Col. F

Cumulation of col. D values.

Col. G

Cumulative Axis occupation payments.
Based on data from B of E, OV 80 20. Memorandum on Greek Finance, 16.

Dec. 1943 interpolated where necessary to end of month values, or interpolated geometrically between months.

Col. H

Cumulative occupation payments to Italy.
= Payments to Axis - payments to Germany.

Col. I

For 9/42, total occupation payment for the month (see note 1) less payment for 9/42 to Germany. Using Xydis' figures to July 1942, Sept. 1942 to Aug. 1943 taking monthly increments in col. (H); Aug. 1942: interpolating. For Sept. 1943, taking note (4) figure and subtracting payment to Germany, possibly indicating a small recovery by the Bank of Greece of credits issued to Italy, and cancelled after Italy's surrender.

Col. J

Gold value of occupation payments to Italy. Col I figures divided by exchange rates in Col. (B).

Col. K

Aggregate of cols. E and J figures.

Col. L

Aggregate of cols. D and I figures.

Col. M

Data from Hahn, *Griechische Währung*, p. 53.
Col. N: German gold sales.
From December 1943, they are calculated from col. N figure multiplied by the col. K figure.
For September-November 1943, note (3): According to Ritter, "German policy," p. 172, the Wehrmacht "gold action" began with the sale in Nov. '43 of £20,000 gold. However, British reports[333] show £15,000 gold was sold in September and £30,000 in October.

Col. O

Total German expenditure from occupation payments and gold sales.

Table A5. Money supply

month	cost of living excl. rent 1940=1	M1 billion dr.	new money billion dr.	money supply billion dr. of 1940 mid month	new money creation million dr. of 1940
Jan-40	0.927	24			
Feb-40	0.927	25	0.57	26.712	610
Mar-40	0.948	26	0.82	26.853	862
Apr-40	0.958	26	0.49	27.244	508
May-40	0.990	27	0.79	27.030	802
Jun-40	1.000	27	0.12	27.210	124
Jul-40	1.000	27	-0.50	27.021	-500
Aug-40	1.010	28	0.78	26.882	776
Sep-40	1.031	28	0.57	26.995	548
Oct-40	1.042	30	1.92	27.905	1843
Nov-40	1.073	32	2.24	29.029	2092
Dec-40	1.094	34	1.82	30.342	1663
Jan-41	1.146	36	1.78	30.535	1552
Feb-41	1.156	38	1.83	31.819	1579
Mar-41	1.177	41	3.38	33.446	2871
Apr-41	1.198	42	1.05	34.722	879
May-41	1.624	43	0.51	26.113	315
Jun-41	2.473	43	0.54	17.353	220
Jul-41	4.230	42	-0.76	10.122	0
Aug-41	5.495	47	4.23	8.098	769
Sep-41	7.878	51	4.26	6.187	540
Oct-41	10.67	55	4.28	4.967	401
Nov-41	17.85	58	3.26	3.183	183
Dec-41	23.31	68	10.01	2.715	430
Jan-42	27.22	77	8.91	2.674	327
Feb-42	38.09	86	8.72	2.143	229
Mar-42	43.22	100	14.25	2.151	330
Apr-42	59.22	116	15.80	1.823	267
May-42	67.63	135	18.58	1.850	275
Jun-42	85.53	159	24.41	1.712	285
Jul-42	88.13	189	29.38	1.965	333
Aug-42	127.9	229	40.16	1.624	314
Sep-42	143.5	282	53.19	1.770	371
Oct-42	228.5	344	61.75	1.362	270
Nov-42	186.1	394	50.26	1.977	270

and seigniorage

net occupation payments billion dr.	net occupation payments million dr. of 1940	seigniorage for Greek government million dr. of 1940	change in real M1 (%)	month
				Jan-40
		610		Feb-40
		862	0.5	Mar-40
		508	1.5	Apr-40
		802	-0.8	May-40
	0	124	0.7	Jun-40
	0	-500	-0.7	Jul-40
	0	776	-0.5	Aug-40
	0	548	0.4	Sep-40
	0	1843	3.4	Oct-40
	0	2092	4.0	Nov-40
	0	1663	4.5	Dec-40
	0	1552	0.6	Jan-41
	0	1579	4.2	Feb-41
	0	2871	5.1	Mar-41
	0	879	3.8	Apr-41
	0	315	-24.8	May-41
	0	220	-33.5	Jun-41
	0	0	-41.7	Jul-41
4.00	727	42	-20.0	Aug-41
3.89	494	46	-23.6	Sep-41
2.55	239	162	-19.7	Oct-41
1.68	94	89	-35.9	Nov-41
6.94	298	132	-14.7	Dec-41
5.43	199	128	-1.5	Jan-42
5.79	152	77	-19.9	Feb-42
6.73	156	174	0.4	Mar-42
8.46	143	124	-15.2	Apr-42
14.26	211	64	1.5	May-42
20.67	242	44	-7.5	Jun-42
18.72	212	121	14.8	Jul-42
19.39	152	162	-17.4	Aug-42
23.00	160	210	9.0	Sep-42
25.87	113	157	-23.0	Oct-42
29.80	160	110	45.1	Nov-42

table A5 (seigniorage) continued

month	cost of living excl. rent 1940=1	M1 billion dr.	new money billion dr.	money supply billion dr. of 1940 mid month	new money creation million dr. of 1940
Dec-42	130.1	437	43.36	3.189	333
Jan-43	132.6	464	26.61	3.397	201
Feb-43	118.6	513	48.86	4.111	412
Mar-43	132.7	619	106	4.245	799
Apr-43	170.1	732	113	3.958	667
May-43	163.0	817	85	4.744	520
Jun-43	178.2	933	116	4.898	649
Jul-43	213.9	1118	185	4.773	864
Aug-43	267.4	1326	209	4.553	780
Sep-43	309.7	1569	243	4.658	784
Oct-43	514.7	2015	446	3.455	867
Nov-43	924.6	2598	583	2.475	630
Dec-43	1212	3503	905	2.489	747
Jan-44	3105	4305	802	1.251	258
Feb-44	4484	5597	1292	1.095	288
Mar-44	12639	8468	2871	0.545	227
Apr-44	17338	18511	10043	0.722	579
May-44	45147	33108	14597	0.548	323
Jun-44	110639	69096	35988	0.432	325
Jul-44	244156	130816	61720	0.389	253
Aug-44	1548398	555959	425143	0.174	275
Sep-44	31229105	7223939	6667980	0.064	214
Oct-44	2.361E+09	725000540	717776601	0.031	304
Nov-44	1.110E+11	6.81E+10	6.737E+10	0.063	605
Dec-44	7.931E+11	1.1E+11	4.19E+10	0.109	53
Jan-45	4.311E+11	2.531E+11	1.431E+11	0.387	332
Feb-45	3.637E+11	4.553E+11	2.022E+11	0.933	556
Mar-45	3.146E+11	6.516E+11	1.963E+11	1.731	624
Apr-45	4.190E+11	1.088E+12	4.359E+11	2.009	1040
May-45	5.859E+11	1.336E+12	2.484E+11	2.057	424
Jun-45	6.085E+11	1.591E+12	2.549E+11	2.396	415
Jul-45	5.526E+11	1.778E+12	1.867E+11	3.043	338
Aug-45	5.596E+11	2.039E+12	2.613E+11	3.402	467
Sep-45	8.132E+11	2.496E+12	4.572E+11	2.774	562
Oct-45	1.285E+12	3.247E+12	7.508E+11	2.216	584

net occupation payments billion dr.	net occupation payments million dr. of 1940	seigniorage for Greek government million dr. of 1940	change in real M1 (%)	month
34.33	264	69	61.3	**Dec-42**
61.68	465	-265	6.5	**Jan-43**
76.32	643	-231	21.0	**Feb-43**
43.00	324	475	3.2	**Mar-43**
51.15	301	366	-6.8	**Apr-43**
57.10	350	170	19.9	**May-43**
64	358	291	3.2	**Jun-43**
144	673	191	-2.5	**Jul-43**
182	681	100	-4.6	**Aug-43**
104	336	449	2.3	**Sep-43**
175	340	527	-25.8	**Oct-43**
290.9	315	316	-28.4	**Nov-43**
440.0	363	384	0.6	**Dec-43**
710.0	229	29	-49.7	**Jan-44**
1280	285	3	-12.5	**Feb-44**
3040	241	-13	-50.2	**Mar-44**
8900	513	66	32.6	**Apr-44**
12700	281	42	-24.1	**May-44**
24000	217	108	-21.2	**Jun-44**
47450	194	58	-9.9	**Jul-44**
246000	159	116	-55.3	**Aug-44**
1320368	42	171	-63.2	**Sep-44**
1800000	0.76	303	-52.2	**Oct-44**
			105.9	**Nov-44**
			72.9	**Dec-44**
			254.7	**Jan-45**
			141.1	**Feb-45**
			85.5	**Mar-45**
			16.0	**Apr-45**
			2.4	**May-45**
			16.4	**Jun-45**
			27.0	**Jul-45**
			11.8	**Aug-45**
			-18.5	**Sep-45**
			-20.1	**Oct-45**

table A5 (seigniorage) continued

month	cost of living excl. rent 1940=1	M1 billion dr.	new money billion dr.	money supply billion dr. of 1940 mid month	new money creation million dr. of 1940
Nov-45	2.051E+12	4.009E+12	7.623E+11	1.759	372
Dec-45	3.877E+12	5.431E+12	1.422E+12	1.204	367
Jan-46	8.291E+12	6.869E+12	1.437E+12	0.737	173
Feb-46	7.117E+12	1.154E+13	4.672E+12	1.251	656
Mar-46	7.271E+12	1.474E+13	3.204E+12	1.794	441
Apr-46	7.427E+12	1.930E+13	4.556E+12	2.271	613
May-46	7.519E+12	2.101E+13	1.705E+12	2.678	227
Jun-46	7.536E+12	2.222E+13	1.215E+12	2.867	161
Jul-46	7.484E+12	2.437E+13	2.145E+12	3.109	287
Aug-46	7.253E+12	2.729E+13	2.925E+12	3.555	403
Sep-46	7.493E+12	2.838E+13	1.090E+12	3.714	145
Oct-46	7.726E+12	2.847E+13	9E+10	3.679	12
Nov-46	8.016E+12	2.667E+13	-1.8E+12	3.438	-225
Dec-46	7.553E+12	3.027E+13	3.595E+12	3.762	476

net occupation payments billion dr.	net occupation payments million dr. of 1940	seigniorage for Greek government million dr. of 1940	change in real M1 (%)	month
			-20.6	Nov-45
			-31.6	Dec-45
			-38.8	Jan-46
			69.8	Feb-46
			43.4	Mar-46
			26.6	Apr-46
			17.9	May-46
			7.0	Jun-46
			8.5	Jul-46
			14.3	Aug-46
			4.5	Sep-46
			-0.9	Oct-46
			-6.6	Nov-46
			9.4	Dec-46

Table A6. Real wages and

month	cost of living including rent	SALARIES AND WAGES: Agapitides index			money salaries and wages at current prices		
		civil servant	private employee	unskilled worker	civil servant	private employee	unskilled worker
1940	1	1	1	1	3800	4000	1508
Jan-41	1.056	1	1	1	3800	4000	1508
Feb-41	1.060	1	1	1	3800	4000	1508
Mar-41	1.104	1	1	1	3800	4000	1508
Apr-41	1.135	1	1	1	3800	4000	1508
May-41	1.424	1	1	1	3800	4000	1508
Jun-41	2.001	1	1	1	3800	4000	1508
Jul-41	3.195	1.48	1.4	1.19	5624	5600	1795
Aug-41	4.055	1.48	1.4	1.72	5624	5600	2594
Sep-41	5.674	1.48	1.4	1.72	5624	5600	2594
Oct-41	7.574	1.48	1.4	1.72	5624	5600	2594
Nov-41	12.45	1.48	2.1	1.72	5624	8400	2594
Dec-41	16.16	1.48	2.1	2.15	5624	8400	3242
Jan-42	18.82	1.97	2.1	2.41	7486	8400	3634
Feb-42	26.20	2.96	2.57	3.62	11248	10280	5459
Mar-42	29.69	2.96	2.8	3.62	11248	11200	5459
Apr-42	40.57	2.96	2.8	3.62	11248	11200	5459
May-42	46.28	2.96	2.8	3.62	11248	11200	5459
Jun-42	58.44	5.79	5.08	2.9	22002	20320	4373
Jul-42	60.21	5.79	7.61	5.43	22002	30440	8188
Aug-42	87.23	5.79	11.42	10.19	22002	45680	15367
Sep-42	97.82	22.38	27.21	11.64	85044	108840	17553
Oct-42	155.9	22.38	31.98	12.54	85044	127920	18910
Nov-42	127.1	22.38	42.22	15.51	85044	168880	23389
Dec-42	89.08	22.38	42.22	15.51	85044	168880	23389
Jan-43	90.74	32.17	42.22	15.51	122246	168880	23389
Feb-43	81.25	32.17	73.31	16.85	122246	293240	25410
Mar-43	90.83	32.17	73.31	18.62	122246	293240	28079
Apr-43	116.5	32.17	73.31	18.62	122246	293240	28079
May-43	111.7	41.64	73.31	18.62	158232	293240	28079
Jun-43	122.1	43.9	119.42	26.86	166820	477680	40505
Jul-43	146.3	48.16	119.42	34.14	183008	477680	51483
Aug-43	182.7	71.84	156.01	34.14	272992	624040	51483
Sep-43	211.4	71.84	156.01	43.45	272992	624040	65523
Oct-43	354.6	138.68	287.03	63.07	526984	1148120	95110

salaries in occupied Greece

SAALARIES AND WAGES 1940 prices			food supplements "pre-war" dr.		SALARIES AND WAGES INCLUDING FOOD SUPPLEMENTS			month
civil servant	private employee	unskilled labour	civil servant	private & unskilled	civil servant	private employee	unskilled worker	
3800	4000	1508			3800	4000	1508	1940
3597	3787	1428			3597	3787	1428	Jan-41
3584	3772	1422			3584	3772	1422	Feb-41
3443	3624	1366			3443	3624	1366	Mar-41
3348	3525	1329			3348	3525	1329	Apr-41
2669	2809	1059			2669	2809	1059	May-41
1899	1999	753			1899	1999	753	Jun-41
1760	1753	562			1760	1753	562	Jul-41
1387	1381	640			1387	1381	640	Aug-41
991	987	457			991	987	457	Sep-41
743	739	342			743	739	342	Oct-41
452	675	208			452	675	208	Nov-41
348	520	201			348	520	201	Dec-41
398	446	193			398	446	193	Jan-42
429	392	208			429	392	208	Feb-42
379	377	184			379	377	184	Mar-42
277	276	135			277	276	135	Apr-42
243	242	118			243	242	118	May-42
376	348	75			376	348	75	Jun-42
365	506	136			365	506	136	Jul-42
252	524	176			252	524	176	Aug-42
869	1113	179			869	1113	179	Sep-42
546	821	121			546	821	121	Oct-42
669	1328	184			669	1328	184	Nov-42
955	1896	263			955	1896	263	Dec-42
1347	1861	258			1347	1861	258	Jan-43
1505	3609	313			1505	3609	313	Feb-43
1346	3229	309			1346	3229	309	Mar-43
1049	2516	241			1049	2516	241	Apr-43
1416	2624	251			1416	2624	251	May-43
1367	3913	332			1367	3913	332	Jun-43
1251	3265	352			1251	3265	352	Jul-43
1495	3416	282			1495	3416	282	Aug-43
1291	2951	310			1291	2951	310	Sep-43
1486	3238	268			1486	3238	268	Oct-43

table A6 continued

month	cost of living including rent	SALARIES AND WAGES: Agapitides index			money salaries and wages at current prices		
		civil servant	private employee	unskilled worker	civil servant	private employee	unskilled worker
Nov-43	633.2	188.3	287.0	104.0	715502	1148120	156802
Dec-43	828.5	188.3	287.0	140.0	715502	1148120	211120
Jan-44	2115	254.9	430.5	219.3	968734	1722160	330750
Feb-44	3052	900.5	574.1	280.0	3421976	2296240	422240
Mar-44	8594	1481.3	765.4	373.3	5628978	3061640	562982
Apr-44	11815	3202	1148	560.0	12165966	4592480	844480
May-44	30713	5859	2296	1120	22265986	9184960	1688960
Jun-44	75219	12982	4592	2240	49332740	18369920	3377920
Jul-44	165954	52500	12247	5973	199500000	48988000	9007782
Aug-44	1052281	472640	529500	104660	1.796E+09	2.118E+09	157827280
Sep-44	21222481	7974930	17965000	13521340	3.03E+10	7.186E+10	2.039E+10
Oct-44	1.604E+09	1.094E+09	1.126E+09	1.336E+09	4.159E+12	4.505E+12	2.015E+12
Nov-44	7.562E+10	6.355E+10	7E+10	1.111E+11	2.415E+14	2.800E+14	1.675E+14
Dec-44	5.470E+11	7.850E+10	9.350E+10	1.940E+11	2.983E+14	3.740E+14	2.926E+14

SAALARIES AND WAGES 1940 prices			food supplements "pre-war" dr.		SALARIES AND WAGES INCLUDING FOOD SUPPLEMENTS			month
civil servant	private employee	unskilled labour	civil servant	private & unskilled	civil servant	private employee	unskilled worker	
1130	1813	248			1130	1813	248	Nov-43
864	1386	255			864	1386	255	Dec-43
458	814	156			458	814	156	Jan-44
1121	752	138	194	194	1315	946	332	Feb-44
655	356	66	194	194	849	550	260	Mar-44
1030	389	71	194	194	1224	583	265	Apr-44
725	299	55	194	194	919	493	249	May-44
656	244	45	194	194	850	438	239	Jun-44
1202	295	54	194	194	1396	489	248	Jul-44
1707	2013	150	451	194	2158	2207	344	Aug-44
1428	3386	961	451	323	1879	3709	1284	Sep-44
2593	2808	1256	451	451	3044	3259	1707	Oct-44
3194	3703	2215	451	451	3645	4154	2666	Nov-44
545	684	535	0	0	545	684	535	Dec-44

notes to Table A6.

1) Actual wage, 1940 according to Agapitides:

Civil servant (month) 3,800 dr.

Private employee (month) 4000 dr.

Labourers (day wage) 58 dr.

" work-month" in days, 26

Post-war, government salaries were paid half a month in advance.[334]

2) Payment of wages

1944: pay every 10th day, later every 5th.

Nov. 44 ,government pay every fifth day. Delivanis & Cleveland, *Greek monetary developments*, pp. 93, 109.

Assume: government pay 1/2 months in advance, private pay, in arrears.

Government servants faced prices at the root of the mean of preceding month times the mean of current month, - i.e. at the 1st of the month.

Private employees: to Sep. 44, index as of 10th of the month

Sept. -Nov. 1944, index as of 5th of the month.

Wage in kind: value at moment of wage payment: Delivanis & Cleveland, *Greek monetary developments*, pp. 93-4.

Table A7. Real wages and salaries in liberated Greece

month	cost of living including rent	Bank of Greece wage index	real wages	government salaries secretary "A"	
				current money	real
1940	1	100	100	100	100
Nov-44	7.562E+10	255	71.0	190	53
Dec-44	5.470E+11	239	21.8	190	17
Jan-45	3.766E+11	247	32.8	190	25
Feb-45	3.182E+11	277	43.5	190	30
Mar-45	2.774E+11	327	58.9	290	52
Apr-45	3.678E+11	325	44.2	290	39
May-45	5.123E+11	359	35.0	290	28
Jun-45	5.319E+11	575	54.1	430	40
Jul-45	4.851E+11	577	59.5	430	44
Aug-45	4.912E+11	579	58.9	430	44
Sep-45	7.108E+11	581	40.9	430	30
Oct-45	1.119E+12	1034	46.2	870	39
Nov-45	1.782E+12	1652	46.3	1080	30
Dec-45	3.377E+12	4039	59.8	2160	32
Jan-46	7.198E+12	4706	32.7	3790	26
Feb-46	6.216E+12	5500	44.2		
Mar-46	6.349E+12	5505	43.4		
Apr-46	6.484E+12	9231	71.2		
May-46	6.563E+12	6851	52.2		
Jun-46	6.578E+12	7460	56.7		
Jul-46	6.560E+12	7460	56.9		
Aug-46	6.360E+12	7707	60.6		
Sep-46	6.568E+12	7707	58.7		
Oct-46	6.769E+12	10213	75.4		
Nov-46	7.021E+12	7707	54.9		
Dec-46	6.620E+12	15432	116.6		
11/11/44	1.795E+11				

note

Secretary "A" salary: Delivanis & Cleveland, *Greek monetary developments*, pp. 119, 124, 133, 136.

NOTES

1 E. S. Brezis & F. H. Crouzet, 'The role of the assignats during the French Revolution: An evil or a rescuer?' *Journal of European Economic History*, 24 (1995) pp. 7-40; A. D. White, 'Fiat money inflation in France,' in F. Capie (ed) *Major Inflations in History* (Aldershot, 1991); M. Bordo, 'A tale of two currencies: British and French finance during the Napoleonic wars,' *Journal of Economic History*, 51 (1991).

2 Steven B. Webb, *Hyperinflation and Stabilization in Weimar Germany*. (New York, Oxford: OUP, 1989); C.-L. Holtfrerich, *The German Inflation 1914-23: Causes and effects in International Perspective*. (Berlin, 1986); Gerald D. Feldman *The Great Disorder Politics, Economics, and Society in the German Inflation, 1914-1924* (Oxford, 1993); T. J. Sargent, 'The ends of four big inflations,' in Capie, *Major Inflations*; Niall Ferguson, 'Constraints and room for speculation in the German inflation of the early 1920s,' *Economic History Review* 49 (1996) 4; Elizabeth Boross, *Inflation and Industry in Hungary, 1918-1929* (Berlin, 1994); Z. Landau, 'Inflation in Poland after World War I,' in *Inflation through the Ages*. ed. N. Schmukler & E. Markus, (New York, 1983). An adequate recent synopsis of the main features of the Russian hyperinflation after World War I is provided in Stephany Griffith-Jones, *The Role of Finance in the Transition to Socialism* (London, 1981).

3 W. Bomberger & G. E. Makinen, 'The Hungarian hyperinflation and stabilization of 1945-1946,' *Journal of Political Economy*, 91 (1983); idem, 'Indexation, inflationary finance and hyperinflation: the 1945-6 Hungarian experience,' *Journal of Political Economy*, 88 (1980); Pierre L. Siklos, *War Finance, Reconstruction, Hyperinflation and Stabilization in Hungary 1938-48* (Oxford, 1991).

4 A short but useful analysis of the 1989 and 1992-94 Yugoslav hyperinflations is provided by G. Pitic & B. Dimitrijevic, 'Two Yugoslav Hyperinflations: A Comparative Analysis,' *Industrija* (Belgrade) 22 (1995) pp. 43-70. Mladjan Dinkić's superb polemic work, *Ekonomija destrukcije. Velika pljacka naroda.* [The Economy of Destruction. The great Theft from the Nation] (Belgrade, 1995) has, unfortunately, not been translated.

5 The second Hungarian hyperinflation is represented conventionally as the most extreme in history, but the figures are exaggerated because they measure the extreme inflation of a currency, the regular pengö, after it had been displaced by the tax-pengö and had ceased to circulate.

6 P. Cagan, 'The Monetary Dynamics of Hyperinflation,' in *Studies in the Quantity Theory of Money*. ed. Milton Friedman (Chicago, 1956) pp. 25-117.

7 P. Bernholz, 'Currency substitution during hyperinflation in the Soviet Union 1922-1924', *Journal of European Economic History*, 25 (1996) table 3, p. 318.

8 T. J. Sargent, 'The ends of four big inflations,' in Capie, *Major inflations* pp. 158-9, 191.

9 J. Rostowski and J. Shapiro, *Secondary currencies in the Russian hyperinflation and stabilization of 1921-24*. (Centre for Economic Performance discussion paper no. 59. January 1992) pp. 17-21.

10 V. Tanzi, 'Inflation, Lags in Collection and the Real Value of Tax Revenue,' *I. M. F. Staff Papers*, 24 (1977).

11 A. F. Freris, *The Greek Economy in the Twentieth Century* (London, 1986) p. 117.

12 Sargent, 'Ends of four big inflations,' pp. 152, 199.

153

13 Steven. B. Webb, 'Four ends of the big inflation in Germany after World War I,' in *Monetary Regime Transformations*. ed. Barry Eichengreen. (Aldershot, 1992) pp. 224-251. The substance is embedded in Webb's *Hyperinflation and Stabilization*, pp. 65-74.

14 Harry Ritter, 'German Policy in Occupied Greece and its Economic Impact,' in *Germany and Europe in the Era of the Two World Wars*. ed. F. X. J. Homer & L. D. Wilcox (Charlottesville, 1986).

15 Mogens Pelt, *Tobacco, Arms and Politics. Greece and Germany from World Crisis to World War 1929-41*. (Copenhagen, 1998) esp. pp. 65-82.

16 On the gold reserve, see Bank of Greece, *The Economic Situation in Greece and the Bank of Greece in 1946. Report for the years 1941, 1944, 1945 and 1946.* (Athens, 1948) pp. 8-9. The disappearance of the printing plates is inferred from the expedients subsequently adopted by the occupation authorities, and by the Greek government appointed by them.

17 Expansion of M1 end September 1940 - end March 1941.

18 Comparison is with expansion of real money supply, average of August 1941-September 1944.

19 Bickham Sweet-Escott, *Greece. A political and Economic Survey 1939-1953* (London, 1954) p. 93.

20 Mark Mazower, *Inside Hitler's Greece. The Experience of Occupation, 1941-44* (Yale, 1993) p. 26.

21 Ibid, p. 26.

22 Ibid, pp. 24, 27.

23 Freris, *Greek Economy*, pp. 102-109.

24 Eva Ehrlich, 'Infrastructure' in M. Kaser and E. A. Radice (eds.) *The Economic History of Eastern Europe 1919-1975* (Oxford, 1985) I, p. 372.

25 Stephen G. Xydis, *The Economy and Finances of Greece under Occupation* (New York, n.d. 1945?) p. 42.

26 Gail E. Makinen, 'The Greek Hyperinflation and Stabilization of 1943-1946,' *Journal of Economic History*, XLVI (1986) p. 797.

27 Ibid.

28 G. Karatzas, 'The Greek Hyperinflation and Stabilization of 1943-1946: A Comment on Makinen,' *Journal of Economic History*, 48 (1988) p. 138.

29 PRO T 236 142 Hill, 23 April 1945.

30 Xydis, *Economy and Finances*, p. 43.

31 B of E. OV 80 20. Waight's memorandum on Greek finance. 16 Dec 1943.

32 At 487m. dr. of 1940 a month, at current prices, their issues would have been the exchange equivalent of 790m. dr. in May, 1024m. in June and 2059m. in July.

33 Xydis, *Economy and Finances*, p. 44.

34 Ritter, 'German Policy,' p. 161.

35 Hermann Neubacher, *Sonder-Auftrag sudost 1940-45. Bericht eines fliegenden Diplomaten* (Göttingen, 1957) p. 93.

36 Ritter, 'German Policy,' p. 166.

37 Neubacher, *Sonder-Auftrag*, p. 74.

38 Ritter, 'German Policy', pp. 167, 181.

39 William H. McNeill, *The Greek Di-*

lemma, *War and Aftermath* (London, 1947) p. 43.

40 Kosta Vergopoulos, 'The Emergence of the New Bourgeoisie 1944-1952' in *Greece in the 1940s. A Nation in Crisis.* ed. J. O. Iatrides (Hanover, 1981) p. 302.

41 Neubacher, *Sonder-Auftrag*, p 86.

42 Paul Hahn, *Die griechische Währung und Währungspolitische Massnahmen unter der Besetzung, 1941-1944.* (Tübingen, 1957) p. 28.

43 Ibid, p. 38.

44 Freris, *Greek Economy*, pp. 58-9.

45 Neubacher, *Sonder-Auftrag*, p. 87.

46 Hahn, *Griechische Währung*, p. 51.

47 Ibid, p. 34.

48 S Agapitides and N Pizanias, *To kostos tis stoiheiodous syntiriseos kata tin katohin* (Athens, 1945) p. 17.

49 Neubacher, *Sonder-Auftrag*, p. 93.

50 A good recent account of this operation is available in G. H. B. Franco, 'The Rentenmark miracle' in Eichengreen, *Monetary Regime Transformations.*

51 Neubacher, *Sonder-Auftrag*, p. 91.

52 Hahn, *Griechische Währung*, pp. 53, 58.

53 Xydis, *Economy and Finances*, pp. 24, 27.

54 Mazower, *Hitler's Greece*, p. 38.

55 Neubacher, *Sonderauftrag*, p. 84; Angeliki Laiou-Thomadakis, 'The Politics of Hunger: Economic Aid to Greece, 1943-1945,' *Journal of the Greek Diaspora*, 7 (1980) part 2, p. 29.

56 Dimitrios Delivanis & William C. Cleveland, *Greek Monetary Developments 1939-1948. A Case Study of the Consequences of World War II for the Monetary System of a Small Nation.* (Bloomington, Indiana, 1949) pp. 68, 84 and statistical appendix.

57 Ritter, 'German Policy,' p. 162 and note p. 176.

58 Sweet Escott, *Greece*, p. 93.

59 B of E. OV 80.21 Hill's memorandum, p. 2.

60 Secret report 26 Sep 1943, in PRO T 160 1265 18214 014 1.

61 April-May 1943 real unskilled day wages on private jobs without food or prospect of stealing. Report of 20 Aug 1943, H12. August unskilled day wages paid by Germans, adjusted for food allowances, in report of 26 Sep 1943; September unskilled wage, see memorandum on Greek finance 16 Dec 1943. All in PRO T 160 1265 18214 014 1.

62 Stavros B. Thomadakis, 'Black Markets, Inflation, and Force in the Economy of Occupied Greece,' in *Greece in the 1940s. A Nation in Crisis.* ed J. O. Iatrides (Hanover, 1981) p. 77.

63 Delivanis and Cleveland, *Greek Monetary Developments*, p. 93.

64 PRO FO 371 43690. R11706. Report dated 13 Jul 1944, fo. 164.

65 Delivanis & Cleveland, *Greek Monetary Developments*, p. 95.

66 J. O. Iatrides, *Ambassador MacVeagh*

Reports. Greece 1933-47. (Princeton, 1960) pp. 631, 635.

67 PRO FO 371 43726. R21396, 'Review of the present currency situation in Greece ... 13 Nov 1944,' ff. 92, 93, 96.

68 Gardner Patterson, 'The Financial Experience of Greece from Liberation to Truman Doctrine (October 1944 - March 1947)' Unpublished PhD Thesis, Harvard University, 1948. p. 26.

69 PRO FO 371 43724 Leeper, 7 Nov 1944.

70 PRO FO 371 43724 Leeper, 22 Oct 1944, fo. 49.

71 Delivanis and Cleveland, *Greek Monetary Developments*, p. 94.

72 Thomadakis, 'Black Markets,' pp. 77-78.

73 Laiou-Thomadakis, 'Politics of Hunger,' p. 29.

74 PRO FO 371 45693 despatches by Leeper R16002 and R16218 of 30 Sep 1944, and R15882 of 5 Oct 1944.

75 B of E. OV 80 21. fo. 182 Cypher F5/P/317 of 21 Oct 1944.

76 Delivanis and Cleveland, *Greek Monetary Developments*, p. 98.

77 John O. Iatrides, *Revolt in Athens* (Princeton, 1972) p. 144.

78 Christos Hadziossif, 'Economic stabilization and political unrest. Greece 1944-1947,' in Lars Baerentzen, J. O. Iatrides, O. L. Smith, eds. *Studies in the History of the Greek Civil War 1945-1949.* (Copenhagen, 1987) pp. 32-3.

79 B of E. OV 80 21. Memorandum by Henry A. Hill commenting on reports received from inside Greece on the status of Greek banks. 1 Aug 1944, p. 9.

80 B of E. OV 80 21. Hill memorandum, p. 13.

81 Neubacher, *Sonder-Auftrag*, p. 80.

82 PRO FO 371 48426 Memorandum on unemployment in Greece by W. J. Hull, labour attaché at the embassy. Cover of 3 May 1945.

83 Harold Macmillan, *The Blast of War, 1939-1945.* (London, 1967) p. 588.

84 *The Collected Writings of John Maynard Keynes*. Ed. D. E. Moggridge, (London, 1980) XXIII, pp. 30-31.

85 Keynes, *Collected Writings*, XXIII, pp. 34-38.

86 Bank of Greece, *Economic situation*, p. 12.

87 B of E. OV 80 20, Waight's memorandum on Greek finance, p. 12.

88 B of E. OV 80 20, Preliminary report on operations in the Dodecanese and Aegean, fo. 109, pp. 2, 3, 7, 8.

89 Wray O Candilis, *The Economy of Greece, 1944-1966.* (New York, 1968) p. 15.

90 Ibid, p. 24.

91 PRO T 160 1265 18217 014 2. Chargé d'Affaires to Greek government - Foreign Office, 6 Sep. 1944, instructions to Varvaressos by Greek finance ministry.

92 Ibid.

93 PRO T 160 1265 18217 014 2. Leeper-FO, 5 Sep. 1944.

94 PRO T 160 1265 18217 014 2 despatch of 6 Sep. 1944.

95 On which, see Candilis, *Economy of Greece*, p. 23. The document however transmits the Finance Ministry's views through Varvaressos to the British.

96 PRO FO 371 43724. R17391, minute of 26 Oct. 1944, financial situation in Greece.

97 PRO T 160 1265 18217 014 2. cypher 5 Sep. 1944.

98 PRO T 160 1265 18217 014 2. Charge d'Affaires to Greek government - Foreign Office, 6 Sep. 1944, instructions to Varvaressos by Greek finance ministry.

99 PRO T 160 1265 18217 014 2. Trevaldwyn-Fraser, 15 Sep. 1944.

100 PRO T 160 1265 18217 014 2. cypher 15 corps 17 Oct. 1944.

101 B of E. OV 80 22. Waley-Treasury, 5 Nov 1944.

102 PRO FO 371 43726. R21396. 'Review ..,' ff. 93-94.

103 Vladimir Petrov, *Money and Conquest. Allied Occupation Currencies in World War 2.* (Baltimore 1967) p. 46 n. 7.

104 Iatrides, *Ambassador MacVeagh Reports*, p. 629.

105 Macmillan, *Blast of War*, p. 589.

106 PRO FO 371 43724. Greekaid-War Office, 20 Oct 1944, fo. 132.

107 Macmillan, *Blast of War*, p. 590.

108 PRO FO 371 43724 Greekaid-War Office, 20 Oct 1944. fo. 132.

109 PRO FO 371 43724 R17640 of 21 Oct 1944.

110 B of E. OV 80 21. Secret 23 Oct 1944. Initialled CPC.

111 B of E. OV 80 21. Waley, Athens, 29 Oct 1944.

112 Macmillan, *Blast of War*, p. 589.

113 Anthony Eden, *The Reckoning*. (London, 1965) p. 489.

114 Macmillan, *Blast of War*, p. 594.

115 Iatrides, *Ambassador McVeagh Reports*, p. 637.

116 B of E. OV 80 21. fo. 229. Cypher. Waley - Treasury, 31 Oct 1944.

117 B of E. OV 80 22. Treasury - Waley, 1 Nov 1944; Patterson, Thesis, pp. 30-31.

118 B of E. OV 80 22. fo. 9. Waley - Treasury, Athens, 2 Nov 1944.

119 Patterson, Thesis, p. 33.

120 B of E. OV 80 22. fo. 29. Waley - Treasury, 5 Nov 1944. No. 136.

121 Eden, *Reckoning*, p. 492; Macmillan, *Blast of War*, p. 594.

122 Macmillan, *Blast of War*, p. 594.

123 PRO FO 371 43725. Minutes of first meeting at the Bank of Greece 4 November.

124 PRO FO 371 43725. FO. 47 Leeper - FO, 9 Nov 1944.

125 Patterson, Thesis, pp. 44-5.

126 PRO FO 371 43725. FO. 47 Leeper - FO, 9 Nov 1944.

127 PRO FO 371 43725. minute of 3rd meeting at Bank of Greece, 7 Nov 1944.

128 Patterson, Thesis, p. 48.

129 Candilis, *Economy of Greece*, p. 26.

130 B of E. OV 80 22. Minutes of third meeting at the Bank of Greece.

131 B of E. OV 80 22. fo. 37E. Zolotas memorandum.

132 See S. S. Katzenellenbaum, *Russian Currency and Banking, 1914-1924* (London, 1925) the probable source of Zolotas' familiarity with the chervonets-sovznak device.

133 PRO T 160 1265 18217 014 2. Despatch of 6 Sep. 1944,

134 B of E. OV 80 22. fo. 125. Jones - Treasury 14 Nov. 1944.

135 B of E. OV 80 22. Minutes of third meeting at the Bank of Greece.

136 B of E. OV 80 22. fo. 41A. Beale - Bank of England, Athens, 7 Nov. 1944.

137 PRO FO 371 43725. Minutes of first meeting at the Bank of Greece, 4 November.

138 B of E. OV 80 22. fo. 65. Minutes of fourth meeting at Bank of Greece, 8 Nov. 1944; fo. 67. Waley - Treasury. Athens, 9 Nov. 1944.

139 B of E. OV 80 22. fo. 145.

140 Patterson, Thesis, pp. 66-7.

141 R. B. Anderson, W. A. Bomberger and G. E. Makinen, 'The Demand for Money, the 'Reform Effect,' and the Money Supply Process in Hyperinflations. The Evidence from Greece and Hungary II Re-examined,' *Journal of Money, Credit and Banking*, 20 (1988) p. 656, suggest that Patterson's 'speculation' that large quantities of 'old' drachmas were issued after stabilization was the result of his working with an excessively low circulation figure of 121 million new drachma equivalent for 10 November, the eve of the 1944 monetary reform. (Patterson's figure independently agrees with Delivanis and Cleveland at this point.) True, the Agapitides November circulation figure rises sharply above the Delivanis and Cleveland figure. Anderson et al. regard Agapitides figures as superior to those of Delivanis and Cleveland, so on this basis they conclude that these 'old' drachmas were probably already in circulation on stabilization day. Unfortunately the Agapitides figures are for the 15th of the month, not the 10th, see Agapitides and Pizanias, *To kostos, pp. 12-13* by which date Patterson shows the money supply to have leapt to 416 million. (Patterson, Thesis, p. 70.) The Anderson et al. analysis therefore fails to upset Patterson's contention that the 'old' drachmas were illegally issued after stabilization. (Patterson, incidentally was not 'speculating:' he was writing as an informed insider, of 'strong indications' that the Greeks were 'in fact' doing what they had wanted to do, but had been told not to do by the British.)

142 B of E. OV 80 22. fo. 70. Waley - Treasury, 9 Nov 1944, no. 183.

143 PRO FO 371 43725. Stabilization of the Greek currency with Sir David Waley's compliments. undated.

144 Ibid.

145 PRO FO 371 43725 fo. 5. Leeper. Cypher undated.

146 PRO FO 371 43725 fo. 24. Athens-FO. Cypher. undated.

147 PRO FO 371 43725. Minutes of 2nd and 3rd meetings at the Bank of Greece, 4 and 6 Nov 1944.

148 PRO FO 371 43726. R21510 Hugh-Jones-Treasury, 21 Dec 1944.

149 PRO T 236 1044. Leeper-FO, 11 Apr 1945.

150 PRO FO 371 43725. Athens, 3 Dec 1944.

151 PRO FO 371 43725. Leeper, 21 Nov 1944, fo. 59.

152 S. Agapitides, 'Wage policy in Greece,' *International Labour Review*, 61 (1950) p. 258.

153 PRO FO 371 43726. R21602. fo. 130.

154 PRO FO 371 43726. R21107 Leeper, 17 Dec 1944.

155 Patterson, Thesis, pp. 84-6.

156 PRO FO 371 43726. R20929, Hugh Jones-Waley, 14 Dec 1944, fo. 58.

157 (Sir) Reginald Leeper, *When Greek Meets Greek*. (London, 1950) p. 158.

158 Patterson, Thesis, pp. 77-8.

159 PRO FO 371 43726. R21107 Waley-Leeper, 27 Dec 1944, ff. 73-4.

160 Patterson, Thesis, pp. 94-5.

161 See table A7.

162 Anderson et al, 'Demand for Money,' pp. 657-8.

163 Iatrides, *Revolt in Athens*, p. 147.

164 PRO FO 371 43726. R21396. Currency situation in Greece, fo. 95.

165 B of E. 80 22. Copy. Presse de 11 Nov. 1944, (*Kathimerina Nea*) fo. 96.

166 PRO FO 371 43726. R21602. MLHQ progress report 11-17 Nov. 1944, fo. 130.

167 B of E. OV 80 22. fo. 145. Hugh Jones-Treasury, 16 Nov 1944.

168 The difference between his figures and mine arises from his use for November of stabilization day prices, which are much higher than the monthly average (used for consistency) in this study. As the discussion below demonstrates, however, neither are a good guide to what actually happened.

169 George Karatzas, 'The Greek Hyperinflation and Stabilization of 1943-1946: a Comment on Makinen,' *Journal of Economic History*, 48 (1988) p. 139. Karatzas refers to the table on pp. 798-9 of Makinen, 'Greek Hyperinflation and Stabilization' [1986].

170 G. E. Makinen, 'The Greek Hyperinflation and Stabilization of 1943-1946: a Reply,' *Journal of Economic History*, 48 (1988) pp. 141-2.

171 Delivanis and Cleveland, *Greek Monetary Developments*, p. 123.

172 G. E. Makinen, 'The Greek Stabilization of 1944-46,' *American Economic Review*, 74 (1984) p. 1068.

173 Gross receipts from aid deliveries over this period were 16.4 billion drachmas, distribution expenses 16.8 billion. Makinen, 'Greek Stabilization' [1984] p. 1069.

174 Karatzas, 'Greek Hyperinflation,' p. 138.

175 Makinen, 'Greek Hyperinflation ...a Reply,' p. 140.

176 Sweet Escott, *Greece*, p. 98.

177 A Lykogiannis, 'The Early Post-War Greek Economy: from Liberation to the Truman Doctrine,' *Journal of European Economic History*, 23 (1994) p. 356.

178 Patterson, Thesis, pp. 47-8.

179 PRO T 236 138 of 10 Mar 1945.

180 S. Agapitides, 'Wage policy in Greece,' *International Labour Review*, 61 (1950) p. 258.

181 Delivanis & Cleveland, *Greek Monetary Developments*, pp. 122, 124.

182 PRO T 236 138. Economic adviser - HM Ambassador, 10 Mar 1945.

183 Hadziossif, 'Economic stabilization,' p. 27.

184 G. M. Alexander, *The Prelude to the Truman Doctrine. British Policy in Greece 1944-1947*. (Oxford, 1982) pp. 95-6.

185 Hadziossif, 'Economic stabilization,' p. 28, citing PRO FO 371 48327, Leeper-FO 13 Feb 1945.

186 PRO T 236 138. Confidential 10 Mar 1945.

187 PRO T 236 1044 Hill-Bridges, 24 Apr 1945.

188 Heinz Richter, *British Intervention in Greece from Varkiza to Civil War*. (London, 1986) p. 83.

189 Patterson, Thesis, p. 104.

190 Richter, *British Intervention*, pp. 83-4.

191 Delivanis & Cleveland, *Greek Monetary Developments*, p. 113.

192 PRO FO 371 43725. fo. 153 Leeper 24 Nov 1944; T 236 1014. Leeper - FO, 4 May 1945, summary of Greek Financial Information.

193 Patterson, Thesis, pp. 168-71.

194 National Bank of Greece, *Reports*, p. 9.

195 Bank of Greece, Monthly Bulletin, Feb 1947, p. 29.

196 A. J. Kondonassis, 'The Greek inflation and the flight from the Drachma 1940-1948,' *Economy and History*, 20 (1977) p. 44.

197 Evangelos A. Eliades, 'Stabilization of the Greek Economy and the 1953 Devaluation of the Drachma,' *IMF Staff Papers*, 4, (1954/55) pp. 29-30.

198 Alexander, *Prelude*, pp. 100-106; Leeper, *When Greek Meets Greek*, pp. 160-1.

199 PRO T 236 1044. Hill-Bridges, 24 Apr 1945.

200 Makinen, 'Greek hyperinflation,' [1986] p. 800.

201 PRO T 236 42. Notes of discussions on the revised Greek budget, 3 Aug 1945.

202 Patterson, Thesis, pp. 107-8.

203 PRO T 236 42. Greece. Notes on M. Mantzavinos' Draft Budget; enclosure 2 to letter of Q Hill dated 23 April 1945.

204 PRO T 236 1044. Leeper - FO cypher 4 May 1945.

205 Keynes, *Collected Writings*, XXV, p. 266; XXVI, p. 43.

206 UNRRA. *UNRRA: The History of the UN Relief and Rehabilitation Administration.* (New York, 1950) II, p. 120.

207 PRO T 236 1044. Leeper - FO 1 May 1945.

208 PRO T 236 1044. Varvaressos, statement of April 1945 on the Greek economic situation.

209 PRO T 236 42 Davidson - Hill, 24 May 1945.

210 Bank of Greece. Varvaressos Report. pp. i-ii.

211 Vergopoulos, 'New Bourgeoisie,' p. 306.

212 Ibid, p. 305.

213 Varvaressos report, pp. 244, 263-4.

214 Richter, *British Intervention*, p. 211.

215 Leeper, *When Greek Meets Greek*, p. 181.

216 Makinen, 'Greek Hyperinflation,' [1986] p. 801.

217 PRO T 236 42. Report of C. A. Coombes on the August budgetary estimates of the Greek government, 10 Sep 1945.

218 Patterson, Thesis, p. 190.

219 PRO T 236 42. Coombes, August budgetary estimates.

220 Patterson, Thesis, p. 183.

221 PRO T 236 42 Coombes, August budgetary estimates.

222 Ibid.

223 Patterson, Thesis, p. 188.

224 Ibid, p. 193.

225 Delivanis & Cleveland, *Greek Monetary Developments*, p 133.

226 Patterson, Thesis, p. 181, note 8.

227 Alexander, *Prelude*, p. 124.

228 Procopis Papastratis, 'The purge of the Greek civil service on the eve of the Civil War,' in Baerentzen et al. *Studies in the History of the Greek Civil War*, pp. 51-2.

229 Leeper, *When Greek Meets Greek*, pp. 169-70.

230 McNeill, *Greek Dilemma*, p. 176.

231 PRO T 236 42. Coombes, 10 Sep 1945.

232 Richter, *British Intervention*, pp. 212-3.

233 Patterson, Thesis, p. 228.

234 Delivanis & Cleveland, *Greek Monetary Developments*, pp. 129-140.

235 Patterson, Thesis, p. 244, note 3.

236 Richter, *British Intervention*, p. 213.

237 Alexander, *Prelude*, p. 140.

238 Tanzi, 'Inflation, Lags in Collection,' pp. 154-167.

239 Taking 120 drachmas to the $ on a GDP (see Freris, *Greek Economy*, p. 107) of 64,200 million drachmas.

240 Patterson, Thesis, p. 630.

241 PRO T 236 42. Notes on discussions with the Greek Minister of Finance, 19

and 20 October 1945, annex B. The finances of Greece.

242 Hadziossif, 'Economic Stabilization,' pp. 36-7.

243 Richter, *British Intervention*, p. 296.

244 Alexander, *Prelude*, p. 149.

245 Richter, *British Intervention*, pp. 289, 293, 296-303.

246 Alexander, *Prelude*, p. 149 ff.

247 Ibid, p. 164.

248 Richter, *British Intervention*, p. 359.

249 Delivanis & Cleveland, *Greek Monetary Developments*, p. 138.

250 Eliades, 'Stabilization,' p. 33.

251 Alexander, *Prelude*, p. 165.

252 Leeper, *When Greek Meets Greek*, p. 206.

253 Richter, *British Intervention*, p. 364.

254 B of E. OV 80 26. fo. 124. Memorandum of 7 Jan 1946.

255 B of E. OV 80 26. fo. 152. Cobbold Memorandum dated 23 Jan 1946.

256 B of E. OV 80 26. fo. 95. Confidential draft, 31 Dec 1945.

257 B of E. OV 80 26. fo. 84. Record of a meeting held in Mr. McNeil's room, 24 Dec. [1945]

258 B of E. OV 80 26. Leeper - FO 21 Dec 1945.

259 Ibid.

260 B of E. OV 80 26. fo. 98. Greece. Most Secret. 31 Dec 1945.

261 Ibid.

262 B of E. OV 80 26. Eady-Taylor under cover of Davidson-Bolton, Treasury, 5 Jan 1946.

263 B of E. OV 80 26 fo. 174. Cobbold memorandum, 7 Jan 1946.

264 B of E. OV 80 26. fo. 119. Waley-McNeil, 5 Jan 1946.

265 B of E. OV 80 26. Waley memorandum, 7 Jan 1946.

266 B of E. OV 80 26. fo 84. Greek financial and economic situation. p. 2.

267 B of E. OV 80 26. fo. 124. Cobbold Memorandum, 7 Jan 1946.

268 B of E. OV 80 26. fo. 123. Cobbold memorandum, 7 Jan 1946.

269 B of E. OV 80 26. fo. 170. Note of conversation, Siepmann and Tsouderos, 28 Jan 1946.

270 B of E. OV 80 26. fo. 133. Cobbold - Siepmann, 10 Jan 1946.

271 B of E. OV 80 26. Davidson-Siepmann, 1 Jan 1946, fo. 100.

272 B of E. OV 80 26. Economic-financial situation in Greece, 15 Jan 1945; Richter, *British intervention*, p. 367.

273 Keynes, *Collected Writings*, XXVII, p. 101. Keynes also wanted British troops to be pulled out, and the Greek army to be halved in numbers, since 'it is bound to be useless against Yugoslavia or Russia.' Memorandum of 11 Feb. 1946, Ibid., p. 480.

274 Delivanis & Cleveland, *Greek Monetary Developments*, pp. 143-5.

275 Alexander, *Prelude*, pp. 167-8.

276 Ibid, pp. 176 ff.

277 Patterson, Thesis, p. 535.

278 Eliades, Stabilization,' p. 33.

279 The equivalence at the mint is given in R. G. Hawtrey, *The Gold Standard in Theory and Practice*. (London, 1931) p. 17.

280 Patterson, Thesis, pp. 345-6.

281 McNeill, *Greek Dilemma*, p. 198.

282 Patterson, Thesis, p. 511.

283 Sweet Escott, *Greece*, p 156, deducting 1946 gold sales; Eliades, 'Stabilization,' p. 33.

284 Neubacher, *Sonder-Auftrag*, pp. 87-88.

285 B of E. OV 80 21. fo. 25A. Report on Economic Conditions in Greece up to December 1943, p. 2.

286 B of E. OV 80 23. Memorandum dated 29 Jan 1945, fo. 218.

287 Leeper, *When Greek Meets Greek*, p. 217.

288 Iatrides, *Ambassador McVeagh Reports*, p. 676.

289 PRO FO 371 48426. Memorandum on unemployment, cover of 3 May 1945.

290 PRO FO 371 48446 Economic survey for the week ending 8 Sep. 1945. ff. 179-80.

291 Hadziossif, 'Economic stabilization,' p. 55.

292 Alexander, *Prelude*, pp. 140-45.

293 Papastratis, 'Purge of the Greek Civil Service,' pp. 52-3.

294 An attitude to Greece's 'overgrown and parasitic commercial sector' which was still much alive as late as 1980, see Laiou-Thomadakis, 'Politics of Hunger,' p. 42.

295 A. A. Pallis, *Problems of Resistance in the Occupied Countries*. (London, 1947) p. 16.

296 Vergopoulos, 'New bourgeoisie.'

297 PRO FO 371 43726. R21396 fo. 94.

298 PRO T 236 42. Davidson - Hill, 24 May 1945.

299 PRO T 236 42. Memo on currency, 28 Aug 1945.

300 Eliades, 'Stabilization,' p. 33; Delivanis & Cleveland, *Greek Monetary Developments*, p. 98; Hahn, *Griechische Währung*, p. 58.

301 Bank of Greece, *Economic Situation*, pp. 46-8.

302 Makinen, 'Greek Hyperinflation,' [1986] pp. 798-9.

303 Bank of Greece, *Economic Situation*, p. 48.

304 Patterson, Thesis, p. 544.

305 Ibid, p. 574.

306 For Hungary, 1946, see Bertrand Nogaro, 'Hungary's Recent Monetary Crisis and its Theoretical Meaning,' *American Economic Review*, 38 (1948) p. 536, note 15; goods were also withdrawn from the market for the same purpose, P. Falush, 'Hyperinflation and Currency

Depreciation 2. The Monetary Collapse of Hungary,' *International Currency Review*, 8 No. 5 (1972) p. 57. For Yugoslavia 1992-3 see M. R. Palairet, 'How Long Can the Milošević Regime Withstand Sanctions?' *RFE reports*, 2, 34 (27 August, 1993) p. 23.

307 Patterson, Thesis, pp. 541-2, 303.

308 Ibid, p. 563.

309 Delivanis & Cleveland, *Greek Monetary Developments*, p. 175.

310 S. Agapitides, 'The Inflation of the Cost of Living and Wages in Greece during the German Occupation,' *International Labour Review*, 52 (1945) pp. 643-51.

311 S. Agapitides and N. Pizanias, *To kostos tis stoiheiodous syntiriseos kata tin katohin.* (Athens, 1945) p. 22.

312 Delivanis & Cleveland, *Greek Monetary Developments*, Statistical appendix.

313 Patterson, Thesis, p. 28.

314 Anderson et al., 'Demand for Money,' p. 656.

315 Agapitides & Pizanias, *Kostos*, pp. 12-13.

316 See discussion above p. 63 and note 141 of the problems addressed in this article.

317 Bank of Greece, *Minaion statistikon Deltion*, Novembrios 1946, table 3.

318 Patterson, Thesis, p. 466, 70, 135.

319 PRO T 160 1265 18214 014 1. GHQ, Middle East Forces to War Office, 20 Apr 1944.

320 Hahn, Griechische Währung, p. 18.

321 See deposits in table 9 of Minaion statistikon deltion, Novembrios 1946, column for 'deposits under Private Law'.

322 Patterson, Thesis, p. 466.

323 Xydis, *Economy and Finances*, p. 44.

324 Hahn, *Griechische Wahrung*, p. 41.

325 Ibid, p. 22.

326 Ibid, p. 28.

327 National Bank of Greece, *Reports for the Years 1941-1945 of the Governor ...* (Athens, n.d.) p. 40.

328 Bank of Greece, *Economic situation*, p. 102.

329 Hahn, *Griechische Währung*, p. 53.

330 Patterson, Thesis, p. 267.

331 PRO T 160 1265 18214 014 1. Report H28 of 26 Sep 1943.

332 For salaries of Secretary 'A' grade civil servants see Delivanis and Cleveland, *Greek Monetary Developments*, pp. 119, 124, 133, 136.

333 B of E, OV 80.21, fo.25A (2).

334 Patterson, Thesis, p. 267.

BIBLIOGRAPHY
Documents

Bank of England. [B of E] Overseas department (OV)
80 20, 80 21, 80 22, 80 23, 80 26.

Bank of Greece

Kyriakos Varvaressos, Varvaressos report. Athens, Jan 5, 1952. Mimeo.
Trapeza tis Ellados [Bank of Greece] Minaion Statistikon Deltion, Noembrios 1946. (Athens, 1946). Mimeo.

Public Record Office, London [PRO]

-Treasury [T]

160 1265 18214 014 1, 160 1265 18217 014 2, 236 42, 236 138, 236 142, 236 1014, 236 1044.

-Foreign Office [FO 371]

43690, 43724, 371 43725, 43726, 45693, 48327, 48426, 48446.

Published works and theses

S. Agapitides, 'Wage policy in Greece,' *International Labour Review*, 61 (1950).

S. Agapitides, 'The Inflation of the Cost of Living and Wages in Greece during the German Occupation,' *International Labour Review*, 52 (1945).

S. Agapitides and N. Pizanias, *To kostos tis stoiheiodous syntiriseos kata tin katohin*. (Athens, 1945).

G[eorge] M[artin] Alexander, *The Prelude to the Truman Doctrine: British Policy in Greece 1944-1947*. (Oxford: Clarendon, 1982).

R. B. Anderson, W. A. Bomberger and G. E. Makinen, 'The Demand for Money, the 'Reform Effect,' and the Money Supply Process in Hyperinflations. The Evidence from Greece and Hungary II Re-examined.' *Journal of Money, Credit and Banking*, 20 (1988).

Bank of Greece, *Bulletin of the Bank of Greece, December 1941*.

Bank of Greece, *The Economic Situation in Greece and the Bank of Greece in 1946*. Report for the years 1941, 1944, 1945 and 1946. (Athens, 1948).

Bank of Greece, *Monthly Bulletin*, Feb. 1947.

P. Bernholz, 'Currency substitution during hyperinflation in the Soviet Union 1922-1924', *Journal of European Economic History*, 25 (1996).

Phillip Cagan, 'The Monetary Dynamics of Hyperinflation,' in *Studies in the Quantity Theory of Money*. ed. Milton Friedman (Chicago, 1956).

Wray O. Candilis, *The Economy of Greece, 1944-1966*. (New York: Praeger, 1968).

Dimitrios Delivanis & William C. Cleveland, *Greek Monetary Developments 1939-1948: A Case Study of the Consequences of World War II for the Monetary System of A Small Nation*. (Bloomington: Indiana UP, 1949).

(Sir) Anthony Eden, *The Reckoning*. (London: Cassell, 1965).

Eva Ehrlich, 'Infrastructure' in M. Kaser and E. A. Radice (eds.) *The Economic History of Eastern Europe 1919-1975*. (Oxford: Clarendon, 1985) Vol. I.

Evangelos A. Eliades, 'Stabilisation of the Greek Economy and the 1953 Devaluation of the Drachma,' *IMF Staff Papers*, 4, (1954/55).

A. F. Freris, *The Greek Economy in the Twentieth Century*. (London: Croom Helm, 1986).

Christos Hadziossif, 'Economic stabilisation and political unrest. Greece 1944-1947,' in Lars Baerentzen, J. O. Iatrides, O. L. Smith, eds. *Studies in the History of the Greek Civil War 1945-1949*. (Copenhagen: Museum Tusculanum Press, 1987).

Paul Hahn, *Die griechische Währung und Währungspolitische Massnahmen unter der Besetzung, 1941-1944*. (Tübingen: Studien des Instituts für Besatzungfragen in Tübingen zu den Deutschen Besetzungen im 2. Weltkrieg nr. 10, 1957).

John O. Iatrides, *Ambassador MacVeagh Reports. Greece 1933-47*. (Princeton, 1960).

John O. Iatrides, *Revolt in Athens*. (Princeton: University Press, 1972).

George Karatzas, 'The Greek Hyperinflation and Stabilization of 1943-1946: a Comment on Makinen,' *Journal of Economic History*, 48 (1988).

S. S. Katzenellenbaum, *Russian Currency and Banking, 1914-1924*. (London, 1925).

J. M. Keynes, *The Collected Writings of John Maynard Keynes*. Ed. D. E. Moggridge, (London: Macmillan, 1980) vols. XXIII, XXV, XXVI, XXVII.

A. J. Kondonassis, 'The Greek inflation and the flight from the Drachma 1940-1948,' *Economy and History*, 20 (1977).

Angeliki Laiou-Thomadakis, 'The Politics of Hunger: Economic Aid to Greece, 1943-1945,' *Journal of the Greek Diaspora*, 7 (1980) part 2 pp. 27-42.

(Sir) Reginald Leeper, *When Greek Meets Greek*. (London: Chatto, 1950).

A. Lykogiannis, 'The Early Post-War Greek Economy: from Liberation to the Truman Doctrine,' *Journal of European Economic History*, 23 (1994).

(Sir) Harold Macmillan, *The Blast of War, 1939-1945*. (London: Macmillan, 1967).

Gail E. Makinen, 'The Greek Hyperinflation and Stabilization of 1943-1946,' *Journal of Economic History*, 46 (1986).

Gail E. Makinen, 'The Greek Stabilization of 1944-46,' *American Economic Review*, 74 (1984).

Gail E. Makinen, 'The Greek Hyperinflation and Stabilization of 1943-1946: a Reply,' *Journal of Economic History*, 48 (1988).

Mark Mazower, *Inside Hitler's Greece: The Experience of Occupation, 1941-44*. (Yale UP, 1993).

William H. McNeill, *The Greek Dilemma, War and Aftermath*. (London: Gollancz, 1947).

National Bank of Greece, *Reports for the Years 1941-1945 of the Governor* ... (Athens, n.d.)

Hermann Neubacher, *Sonder-Auftrag südost 1940-45. Bericht eines fliegenden Diplomaten*. (Göttingen: Musterschmidt, 2nd ed. 1957).

A. A. Pallis, *Problems of Resistance in the Occupied Countries*. (London: St. Clements, 1947).

Procopis Papastratis, 'The purge of the Greek civil service on the eve of the Civil War,' in Baerentzen et al. *Studies in the History of the Greek Civil War*.

Gardner Patterson, 'The Financial Experience of Greece from Liberation to Truman Doctrine (October 1944 - March 1947)' Unpublished PhD Thesis, Harvard University, 1948.

Mogens Pelt, *Tobacco, Arms and Politics: Greece and Germany from World Crisis to World War 1929-41*. (Copenhagen: Museum Tusculanum, 1998)

Vladimir Petrov, *Money and Conquest: Allied Occupation Currencies in World War 2*. (Baltimore, 1967)

Heinz Richter, *British Intervention in Greece from Varkiza to Civil War*. (London: Merlin, 1986).

Harry Ritter, 'German Policy in Occupied Greece and its Economic Impact,' in *Germany and Europe in the Era of the Two World Wars*. ed. F. X. J. Homer & L. D Wilcox (Charlottesville: UP of Virginia, 1986).

J. Rostowski and J. Shapiro, *Secondary currencies in the Russian hyperinflation and stabilization of 1921-24*. Centre for Economic Performance discussion paper no. 59. January 1992.

T. J. Sargent , 'The ends of four big inflations,' in Forrest C. Capie, ed. *Major inflations in History*. (Aldershot: Elgar, 1991).

Bickham Sweet-Escott, *Greece: A political and Economic Survey 1939-1953*. (London: RIIA, 1954).

V. Tanzi, 'Inflation, Lags in Collection and the Real Value of Tax Revenue,' *I. M. F. Staff Papers*, 24 (1977).

Stavros B. Thomadakis , 'Black Markets, Inflation, and Force in the Economy of Occupied Greece,' in *Greece in the 1940s: A Nation in Crisis*. ed. J. O. Iatrides (Hanover: U P of New England, 1981).

UNRRA. *UNRRA: The History of the UN Relief and Rehabilitation Administration*. (New York, 1950) II.

Kosta Vergopoulos, 'The Emergence of the New Bourgeoisie 1944-1952' in *Greece in the 1940s: A Nation in Crisis*. ed. J. O. Iatrides (Hanover, 1981).

Steven B. Webb, *Hyperinflation and Stabilization in Weimar Germany*. (New York, Oxford: OUP, 1989).

Stephen G. Xydis, *The Economy and Finances of Greece under Occupation*. (New York: Greek government office of information, n.d. [1945?]).

INDEX

A
Agapitides, S. 23, 40, 43, 44, 65
Agricultural Bank (Greece) 29
Alexander, G. M. 24
Angelopoulos, Angelos 60, 61, 64, 72
Athens
   battle, Dec. 1944 51, 65, 67, 70, 72, 98
   famine 26, 32, 40
   market 44, 56
   property market 80
   stock exchange 36, 116

B
Bank of England 57, 68, 89, 90, 91
Bank of Greece
   British payments 74
   currency emission 32, 62, 74, 95
   gold purchases 108
   gold sales 22, 36, 68, 89-90, 93
   governor 53, 55, 61, 73, 75, 105
   in Battle of Athens 67
   Nov. 1944 negotiations 60
   occupation payments 27, 31, 35, 36
   policy 51, 53, 56
   prestige 91
   reserves 63, 64
   salaries 42, 116
   Samos 52
Beale, Sir Louis 57, 62
Bevin, Ernest 90

C
Cagan, Phillip 10, 16, 17, 22, 25, 70
capital levy 28, 81
Cassa Mediterranea 31
chervonets 13, 14, 15, 62
Churchill, Winston 57
civil service, Greek 43, 46, 58, 64, 79, 81, 82, 84, 97, 99-100, 107, 116, 170
Coombes, Charles 81
Currency Committee (Greece) 24, 95, 106

D
Damaskinos, Archbishop 88, 89
DEGRIGES 34
Delivanis & Cleveland 22, 23, 47

E
Eady, Sir Wilfrid 90
Eden, Sir Anthony 57, 60, 73
ELAS 40, 47, 51, 65-69, 75

F
famine 26, 40
Fisher equation 12, 54, 56
Foreign Office (British) 54, 64, 89-91, 93

G
gold action 37, 47, 57, 59, 65, 141
Göring, Hermann 38
Grove, adviser to Foreign Office 90, 91

H
Hahn, Paul 23, 37, 97, 113
Hitler, Adolf 38
Hungary, hyperinflation, 1944-46 14, 26, 107, 169

K
Kanellopoulos, Panayotis 88
Karatzas, George 28, 69, 70, 72
Kartalis, Georgios 89
Kasimatis, Gregorios 88-89
Keynes, J. M. 51, 77, 92, 167

L
Lahiri, A. K. 18
Leeper, Sir Rex 24, 64, 71, 75, 77, 82, 88-90, 98, 99
liberation drachma 53, 62

M
Macmillan, Harold 51, 56-58, 60, 64, 72
Makinen, Gail 6, 24, 27, 56, 69-72, 75, 80, 105, 161
Mantzavinos, Georgios A. 62, 75-77, 105, 106
Mazower, Mark 23
McNeil, Hector 90
McNeill, W. H. 94
McVeagh, Lincoln, US ambassador to Greece 58, 98
Metaxas, Ioannis 25, 53, 64
Military Liaison 72
Mylonas, Alexandros 75
Mytilene island 34

N
National Bank of Greece 42, 62
National Guard 55, 67, 72
National Product, Greece 27
Neubacher, Hermann, Reich special commissioner in Greece 19, 23, 32, 33-39, 42, 57, 59, 70, 88, 94, 96-97, 105

O

occupation levy 23, 27, 29-33, 35-38, 56, 96, 114-116
olive oil 14, 34, 44, 45, 52, 80, 83

P

Papandreou, Georgios 51, 56, 60, 64
Paraskevopoulos, Ioannis 87
parties, Greece
    E.A.M. 43, 46, 47, 53, 60, 64, 98
    Liberal 73
    Royalists 89, 93, 94
partisans 33, 36, 38, 47, 52, 101
Patterson, Gardner 24, 61, 73, 80, 81, 82, 84, 95, 96, 106, 108, 161
Plastiras, Nikolaos 71, 73, 75, 98

R

Rallis, Ioannis, 3rd. occupation premier 38, 44
Red Cross 33, 42
Reichskreditkassenschein 31
Reichsmark 32
Rentendrachma scheme, 1944 38, 96
reparations, against Germany 5, 87
Ribbentrop, Joachim von, Reich Foreign Minister 34, 38
Richter, Heinz 24
Ritter, Harry 23
Rostowski, Jacek 14

S

Samos island, 1943 52, 55
Sandstrom, Dr. (I.R.C.) 46
Sargent, Thomas 5, 21, 108
Sideris, Georgios 73-75
Sophoulis, Themistocles 88, 93
Soviet inflation, 1921-24 5, 13-15, 62, 93
Special Operations Executive 40
Svolos, Alexandros 60, 61, 63, 64
Sweden 32, 45, 46, 72

T

Tanzi, Vito 20, 87, 89
Thomadakis, Stavros 46
Treasury (Great Britain)
    1944 stabilisation plan 19, 55, 57, 58
    1946 stabilisation 89-93
    and Varvaressos 54, 77, 78, 82
    assistance to Greece 87
Trevaldwyn, J. R. 54
Truman Doctrine 24, 95
Tsaldaris, Konstantinos 94, 99

Tsironikas, Hector 97
Tsouderos, Emmanuel 89, 91, 93
Turkey 26, 32

U
UNRRA 72, 79, 81, 82, 84, 88, 91
utilities 27, 46, 55, 111

V
Varkiza agreement 67, 75
Varvaressos, Kyriakos 20, 21, 28, 52, 73, 75, 76-88, 90, 97, 98, 99, 101, 103, 104
Venizelos, Eleftherios 26
Vergopoulos, Kosta 79
Voulgaris, Petros 75, 76, 77, 79, 87, 88, 99

W
Waley, Sir David 19, 55, 57-59, 60-64, 68-71, 73-75, 90-92, 97
war profiteering 48, 74
Webb, Steven 5, 21
Wehrmacht, in Greece 26, 32-37, 39, 42

X
Xydis, Stephen 28

Y
Yugoslavia, 1992-94 inflation 5, 14, 26, 107, 169

Z
Zolotas, Xenophon 53, 55, 61-63, 65, 68, 73, 160